AMERICAN PROPHETS

AMERICAN PROPHETS

SEVEN RELIGIOUS RADICALS AND THEIR
STRUGGLE FOR SOCIAL AND POLITICAL JUSTICE

ALBERT J. RABOTEAU

PRINCETON UNIVERSITY PRESS
PRINCETON AND OXFORD

TO JOANNE SHIMA RABOTEAU

A constant example of compassion

The Spirit of the Lord God is upon me,
because the Lord has anointed me
to bring good news to the poor;
he has sent me to bind up the brokenhearted,
to proclaim liberty to the captives,
and the opening of the prison to those who are bound;
to proclaim the year of the Lord's favor,
and the day of vengeance of our God;
to comfort all who mourn.

—Isaiah 61:1–2

Is not this the fast that I choose:
to loose the bonds of wickedness,
to undo the straps of the yoke,
to let the oppressed go free,
and to break every yoke?
Is it not to share your bread with the hungry
and bring the homeless poor into your house;
when you see the naked, to cover him,
and not to hide yourself from your own flesh?
Then shall your light break forth like the dawn,
and your healing shall spring up speedily;
your righteousness shall go before you;
the glory of the Lord shall be your rear guard.
Then you shall call, and the Lord will answer;
you shall cry, and he will say, "Here I am."
If you take away the yoke from your midst,
the pointing of the finger, and speaking wickedness,
if you pour yourself out for the hungry
and satisfy the desire of the afflicted,
then shall your light rise in the darkness
and your gloom be as the noonday.

And the Lord will guide you continually
and satisfy your desire in scorched places
and make your bones strong;
and you shall be like a watered garden,
like a spring of water,
whose waters do not fail.
And your ancient ruins shall be rebuilt;
you shall raise up the foundations of many generations;
you shall be called the repairer of the breach,
the restorer of streets to dwell in.

— Isaiah 58:6–12

But let justice roll down like waters, and righteousness
like an ever-flowing stream.

—Amos 5:24

Truly, I say to you, as you did it to one of the least of
these my brothers, you did it to me.

—Matthew 25:40

⌐ CONTENTS ⌐

☞ ACKNOWLEDGMENTS ☜

I WISH TO THANK ALL OF YOU WHO took my Religious Radicals course over several years for your interest and inspiration. I learned a lot from you. Translations of Abraham Joshua Heschel's poems are from Abraham Joshua Heschel, *The Ineffable Name of God: Man*, translated by Morton Leifman, © 2004, and Continuum US, an imprint of Bloomsbury Publishing Inc. Other extended quotations from the works of Abraham Joshua Heschel are reprinted with the gracious permission of his daughter, Dr. Susannah Heschel. Excerpts from "On Prayer" from *Moral Grandeur and Spiritual Audacity* by Abraham Joshua Heschel. Copyright © 1996 Sylvia Heschel. Reprinted by permission of Farrar, Straus and Giroux, LLC. The A. J. Muste Institute generously granted permission to reproduce selections from *The Essays of A. J. Muste*, edited by Nat Hentoff, © 2002, the A. J. Muste Memorial Institute. The poem "I Think Continually of Those Who Were Truly Great," from *New Collected Poems of Stephen Spender*, © 2004, is reprinted with kind permission of the Estate of Stephen Spender. For permission to reprint extended selections from Fannie Lou Hamer's speeches, I am indebted to Mrs. Hamer's daughter, Mrs. Vergie Hamer Faulkner. Excerpts from "Foreword" from *Stranger at the Gates* by Tracy Sugarman, with a foreword by Fannie Lou Hamer. Copyright © 1966 by Tracy Sugarman. Reprinted by permission of Hill & Wang, a division of Farrar, Straus and Giroux, LLC. A quotation from *Selma, Lord, Selma: Girlhood Memories of the Civil Rights Days* by Sheyann Webb and Rachel West Nelson, as told to Frank Sikora, © 1980 by the University of Alabama Press, is used by permission. Chapter

4 is a revised version of Albert Raboteau, "In Search of Common Ground: Howard Thurman and Religion Community," in *Meaning and Modernity: Religion, Polity, and Self*, edited by Richard Madsen, William M. Sullivan, Ann Swidler, and Steven M. Tipton, © 2002 by the Regents of the University of California and published by the University of California Press. Chapters 5 and 6 are revised versions of chapters previously published in my own book *A Fire in the Bones*, © 1995, Beacon Press. Portions of the Day, Thurman, Merton, and King chapters were presented as the Stone Lectures at Princeton Theological Seminary, October 1–4, 2012. And an earlier version of chapter 6 was presented as the inaugural J.W.C. Pennington Lecture at Heidelberg University on June 14, 2012. I would like to thank the sponsors of both lectures and the audiences for their generous appreciation. My thanks also to the staff at Princeton's Firestone Library for indefatigable assistance, especially Joan Martine and Margaret Kehrer for their help with office space.

I owe a special debt of gratitude to my faculty colleagues in the Religion and African American studies departments for intellectual stimulation and camaraderie over the years, especially to Eddie Glaude Jr. for unstinting support of a fellow Gulf Coast Mississippian; Cornel West, whose prophetic voice continues to speak truth to power and always conveyed personal compassion for me during times of trouble with a quiet exhortation to "Keep strong brother"; Jeffrey Stout, my most perceptive reader, who often reveals aspects of my texts that I had not consciously realized were there; and the departmental staff, Mary Kay Bodnar, Kerry Smith, Patricia Bogdziewicz, Jeffrey Guest, and Lorraine Fuhrman, who help with unparalleled generosity and warmth to humanize the daily bureaucracy of the institution. Finally, I owe a huge thanks to Beth Stroud, graduate student in the Religion department at Princeton, for her tireless assistance in obtaining permissions and word processing the manuscript text, with grace under pressure.

Recently, I was browsing in my local bookstore when two clerks who knew I taught courses in religion confronted me with an urgent question: "What good does religion do in politics?" They were clearly exasperated by some issue of the so-called culture wars featured in the news that morning. As I paused, they added, "In twenty-five words or less." "I don't need twenty-five," I replied. "My answer is Martin Luther King Jr. and"—remembering the key role of local women in the civil rights movement—"Fannie Lou Hamer." They were surprised and then nodded, "OK, but they were exceptions," as if I'd cheated. They were, of course, right. King and Hamer were exceptional, but they also are exemplary of the values of citizenship that we ought to try to emulate. And both were inspired and motivated by the religious institutions and values of African American social Christianity. In both historical paradigms of the role of religion in politics, the mid-nineteenth-century antislavery movement and mid-twentieth-century civil rights movement, whites were enabled to empathize vicariously with the suffering of African Americans through the written or oral witness of escaped slaves, or the visual spectacle of modern demonstrations captured in photographs and on television (and for some in both eras, to literally share it). This kind of empathetic understanding is crucial to "releasing" the efficacy of the redemptive suffering that King and others preached. It makes people aware ("I never knew it was so bad"), troubles or shames their consciences with the dissonance between principle and practice ("How can this happen in the United States?"), and ideally leads them to some level of action ("What can I do about this?").

Had the two clerks allowed me more than twenty-five words, I might have told them about the course I taught for several years to Princeton undergraduates, Religious Radicals, a seminar on twentieth-century Americans who participated in movements of social and political change for religious reasons. That course is the source of this book. The title of the book is based on a definition of the prophet by Rabbi Abraham Joshua Heschel in his classic study *The Prophets*: "An analysis of prophetic utterances shows that the fundamental experience of the prophet is a fellowship with the feelings of God, sympathy with the divine pathos, a communion with the divine consciousness which comes about through the prophet's reflection of, or participation in, the divine pathos. . . . The prophet hears God's voice and feels His heart. He tries to impart the pathos of the message. . . . As an imparter his soul overflows, speaking as he does out of the fullness of his sympathy." He adds that the prophet is one who is impelled to speak because he feels the divine pathos like a "fire in the bones." Different as they were, each of the figures we will consider—Heschel, A. J. Muste, Dorothy Day, Peter Maurin, Howard Thurman, Thomas Merton, Martin Luther King Jr., and Fannie Lou Hamer—was moved to action by a deep compassion for those suffering injustice or oppression, and each succeeded in conveying this compassion to the larger American public through writing, speaking, demonstrating, and/or organizing. By analyzing their theological and ethical positions, and the rhetorical and strategic methods they employed, this book seeks to illuminate how these exemplars of twentieth-century prophecy in the United States persuasively mobilized some of their fellow citizens to commit themselves to movements for social change.

As I write, the news is awash with commemoration of the fiftieth anniversary of the Selma to Montgomery march focused on the Edmund Pettus Bridge, site of the brutal beating of civil rights activists on what has come to be called "Bloody Sunday." Speeches by the first African American president and many others praise the courage of those who endured the beatings, and preach how far the nation has yet to go to achieve its goal of civil equality despite the passage of the Civil Rights Act of 1964. Memory and mourning combine in prophetic insistence on inner change and outer action to reform systemic structures of racism. Once again, crowds symbolically retrace the steps of the marchers, some actually present, across the bridge. Several years ago I had the privilege of visiting Selma with a group of Princeton alumni along with graduate and undergraduate students. After visiting the museum, close to the base of the bridge, the group decided to walk across it. I couldn't. I stood alone as the rest of the group crossed because I had a strong feeling that I didn't need to. Why? Because during our visit to the National Voting Rights Museum and Institute, Joanne Bland, who had been beaten on the bridge as a child, was our guide, offering personal memories. She pointed to a wall covered with cards from previous visitors, sharing their impressions and feelings, and singled out one—a card written by one of the state patrol officers who had beaten the marchers on Bloody Sunday. He expressed remorse at his behavior and asked forgiveness. During the tour, she struck up a conversation with an elderly alumnus in our group. He was a retired Presbyterian minister, hampered now by arthritis, but eager to visit all the sites, as decades ago he had heeded King's nationwide call for clergy to join the demonstrations in Selma. When she heard this, Bland hugged him and told us how important it had been for the black community of Selma to know that they were not alone—that they had support from people like him, from around the country. They both began to weep, moved by the memory of the solidarity in compassion that bridged the gaps of race then and now. Watching this encounter, the rest of the group, including me, was moved to tears as well. It was a moment of shared pathos that transcended time. For me it was the high point of the trip. I no longer needed to cross the bridge.

I hope that the following pages will help readers grasp the divine pathos that moved each of the prophets whose lives and words I discuss. Let us listen to their voices, which echo those of the exemplary figures they turn to for inspiration and validation: the ancient prophets of Israel, Amos, Isaiah, Jeremiah, and Ezekiel; the Gospel sayings of Jesus, especially the Sermon on the Mount, the Beatitudes, and chapter 25 of Matthew; the American antislavery protest of William Lloyd Garrison and Henry David Thoreau; and fellow pacifists Leo Tolstoy and Mahatma Gandhi, to cite the most prominent. Moreover, their voices invoke the biblical narratives of Exodus, the Promised Land, the Good Samaritan, Lazarus and the rich man, and the passion, death, and resurrection of Jesus. Recalling these paradigmatic stories fires their imagination and potentially that of their audiences to envision a god who cares about and intervenes in human history on behalf of the "poor, the widow, and the orphan,"—the oppressed. As theologian and biblical scholar Walter Brueggemann convincingly argues, it is the deployment of this prophetic imagination that makes it possible to create a counterscript to that imagined by the currently hegemonic culture. And it is the heuristic power of these accumulated stories that feeds the moral authority of the prophet, especially when reenacted in the dramatic action of demonstrations and public protest.

I am all too aware that reading about prophets does not automatically lead to action. As the old dictum says, "Those who can't do, teach." But teaching and reading may lead to doing, as I discovered to my great surprise at the close of one of my Religious Radicals seminars. I asked the students to write a short essay on which readings had most challenged them and why. One student, who had been quiet for much of the semester, picked two readings that had especially moved him. The first was a passage from John Perkins's autobiography, *Let Justice Roll Down*, about organizing the black poor in rural Mississippi. A tenant farmer revealed that he was so impressed by Reverend Perkins's words and example that he "put down the bottle." The second passage was Merton's description of his experience on a street corner in Louisville, when he saw within the people passing by a "virginal" still point and realized that "at the center of our being is a point of nothingness which is untouched by sin and by illusion, a point of pure truth, a point or spark which belongs entirely to God, which is never at our disposal, from which God disposes of our lives, which is inaccessible to the fantasies of our mind or the brutalities of our own will." The student said that he had adamantly refused to acknowledge that he was an alcoholic, despite passing out drunk on the street and being arrested. Reading these two passages, he wrote, "turned my life completely around." He entered a twelve-step program and had been asked to speak to several eating clubs at Princeton about the dangers of binge drinking. Unexpectedly, I learned that teaching and reading could inspire "doing."

AMERICAN PROPHETS

Figure 1.1 Abraham Joshua Heschel. Courtesy: CSU Archives / Everett Collection.

CHAPTER 1

ABRAHAM JOSHUA HESCHEL,
PROPHET OF DIVINE PATHOS

If I say, I will not mention him,
or speak any more in his name,
there is in my heart as it were a burning fire
shut up in my bones,
and I am weary with holding it in,
and I cannot.

—Jeremiah 20:9

IT IS FITTING TO BEGIN THIS BOOK with a chapter on Rabbi Abraham Joshua Heschel, whose description of the prophet as one who shares the divine pathos for humanity characterized not only his own life but also those of each of the seven figures who follow. Born on January 11, 1907, in Warsaw, Poland, Heschel, named after his grandfather, was the youngest of six children; he had four sisters and one brother. His mother, Reizel (Perlow) Heschel, and father, Rabbi Moshe Mordechai Heschel, were each descended from distinguished Hasidic rebbes, a family of nobility in the Jewish world. "Yes," he remarked in later years to an interviewer, "I can trace my family back to the late fifteenth century. They were all rabbis. For seven generations, all my ancestors have been Hasidic rabbis."[1] At the age of eight or nine, he began to study the Talmud, the massive collection of rabbinical commentaries and debates. According to his daughter, Susannah, "As a small child he was accorded the princely honors given the families of Hasidic rebbes: adults would rise when he entered the room, even when he was little. . . . He would be lifted onto a table to deliver . . . learned discussions of Hebrew texts. He was considered . . . a genius."[2] His ancestral pedigree did not shelter him, however, from the anti-Semitism of his Polish environment. As he recalled in a 1967 interview with a Benedictine priest, "I have been stoned and beaten up many times in Warsaw by young boys who had just come out of church."[3] When his father died at the age of forty-three during a flu epidemic, Heschel was nine years old. His uncle, Rabbi Alter Israel Shimon Perlow, took over the responsibility of supervising his education.

Hasidic and Kabbalistic spirituality had a profoundly formative as well as lasting influence on the young Heschel's religious experience and worldview. He absorbed the teaching of the Ba'al Shem Tov, the revered founder of Hasidism, that "we are called to see the holy sparks within all created beings . . . and to bring together the sparks to preserve single moments of radiance and keep them alive in our lives, to defy absurdity and despair and to wait for God to say again: Let there be light. And there will be light."[4]

In later years, Heschel fondly described his childhood heritage:

> I was born in Warsaw, Poland, but my cradle stood in Mezbizh (a small town in Ukraine), where the Ba'al Shem Tov (Master of the Good Name), founder of the Hasidic movement, lived during the last twenty years of his life. That is where my father came from, and he continued to regard it as his home. . . . I was named after my grandfather, Reb Abraham Joshua Heschel—"The Apter Rav," and last great rebbe of Mezbizh. He was mar-

velous in all his ways, and it was as if the Ba'al Shem Tov had come to life in him. . . . Enchanted by a wealth of traditions and tales, I felt truly at home in Mezbizh. That little town so distant from Warsaw and yet so near was the place to which my childish imagination went on many journeys.[5]

The adult Heschel would express his lifelong devotion to Hasidism in aphorisms such as "I have one talent and that is the capacity to be tremendously surprised, surprised by life. . . . This is to me the supreme Hasidic imperative," and "The claim that we not only need God but that God needs us is likewise nurtured from Hasidic roots." As Heschel says in his book about Hasidism, *The Earth Is the Lord's*: "The meaning of man's life lies in his perfecting the universe. He has to distinguish, gather, and redeem the sparks of holiness scattered throughout the darkness of the world. This service is the motive of all precepts and good deeds. Man holds the key that can unlock the chains fettering the Redeemer."[6] By the time he was a teenager, Heschel was writing his first articles, short studies in Hebrew, of Talmudic literature, which were published in a Warsaw rabbinical journal, *Sha'arey Torah* (Gates of Torah) in 1922 and 1923. Deciding he wanted exposure to secular knowledge and culture, he left home for high school in Vilna, Lithuania, at the age of seventeen. Vilna was at the time the center of Eastern European Jewish life and culture, a magnet for poets, philosophers, and religious seekers. There he helped organize a club of young Jewish writers and artists called Young Vilna, and composed his first poems. Although he no longer dressed like a Hasid or studied exclusively religious texts, Heschel continued to observe Jewish law and remained proud of his heritage.

Having passed his final high school exams in June 1927, he decided to study in Berlin and enrolled at the age of twenty at the Academy of Scientific Jewish Scholarship, which trained Liberal rabbis and scholars, and at the University of Berlin. In April 1929, Heschel passed the required entrance exams in German language and literature, Latin, mathematics, German history, and geography. He chose philosophy as his major field, with minors in art history and Semitic philology. Down the street from the academy was the Hildesheimer Seminar, the Orthodox rabbinical seminary. Heschel was one of the few students able to move easily between the two institutions. In a private seminar taught by the social philosopher David Koigen, Heschel developed a vision of a traditional Judaism responsive to the contemporary world. In the decade he spent in Berlin (just as Adolf Hitler came to power), he refined philosophical and theological categories with which to explain religious thinking, prophetic inspiration, and Hasidic piety.[7]

In December 1929, he passed the examinations at the academy in Hebrew language, Bible and Talmud, Midrash, liturgy, philosophy of religion, and Jewish history and literature, and in May 1930, he received a prize for a paper he wrote, "Visions in the Bible." He was also appointed as an instructor, lecturing on Talmudic exegesis to the more advanced students. In July 1934, he passed his oral examinations and was granted a rabbinical degree after completing a thesis titled "Aprocrypha, Pseudepigrapha, and Halakah." On February 23, 1933, just three weeks after Hitler seized control of the government, Heschel took oral examinations for his doctorate at the University of Berlin and passed. That same year his first book, a volume of Yiddish poems, *The Ineffable Name of God: Man*, dedicated to his father's memory, was published in Warsaw. Several of his poems foreshadowed major themes in his later theological work and the aphoristic poetic style in which he wrote. For example, "God's Tears" heralds his belief that sharing in the divine pathos for human suffering reverses the usual criteria of social and moral judgment:

God's tears lie on the cheeks
of shamed, weak people
Let me wipe away His lament

He in whose veins there whirls
a quiet shudder before God,
let him kiss the nails of a pauper

To the worm crushed under-foot
God calls out "My holy martyr!"

The sins of the poor are more beautiful
than the good deeds of the rich.

In "God Follows Me Everywhere," he celebrates God's allusive presence intimated by our capacity for wonder and "radical amazement":

God follows me everywhere—
Spins a net of glances around me,
Shines upon my sightless back like a sun.

God follows me like a forest everywhere.
My lips, always amazed, are truly numb, dumb,
Like a child who blunders upon an ancient holy place.

God follows me like a shiver everywhere.
My desire is for rest; the demand within me is: Rise up,
See how prophetic visions are scattered in the streets.

I go with my reveries as with a secret
In a long corridor through the world—
and sometimes I glimpse high above me, the faceless face of God.

God follows me in tramways, in cafes.
Oh, it is only with the backs of the pupils of one's eyes that
one can see
how secrets ripen, how visions come to be.[8]

In December 1932, Heschel had submitted his dissertation, "Prophetic Consciousness," which was approved by his
committee. For reception of the doctoral degree, however,
the university required that the dissertation be published.
Heschel did not have the money to pay for publication and
had to appeal to the dean for repeated delays until finally, in
1936, the Polish Academy of Sciences published it, with the
costs borne by the Erich Reiss Publishing House in Berlin.
In 1937, at the age of thirty, Heschel left Berlin for Frankfurt
to replace Martin Buber as director of a Jewish adult school
since Buber was immigrating to Palestine to escape the inexorably expanding Nazi persecution. In 1938, Gestapo agents
awakened Heschel in the middle of the night. They gave him
two hours to gather his possessions and report to the local
police station as required by a new law ordering the depor-
tation to Poland of all Jewish residents of Germany holding
Polish passports. Loaded down with two heavy suitcases of
books and manuscripts, Heschel boarded a train so overcrowded that he was forced to stand for most of the three-day
journey. At the Polish border, the refugees were confined in
a squalid detention center. Heschel's family eventually managed to arrange for his release. But it was all too clear that
the situation for Jews in Poland was increasingly precarious.

In spring 1939, he received an invitation from Hebrew
Union College in Cincinnati from its president, Julian Morgenstern, to join the faculty—part of Morgenstern's initiative
to save Jewish intellectuals from the Nazis. To escape meant
that Heschel had to leave his family, for whom visas were not

available. That summer, he left for England six weeks before the Nazis invaded Poland. He stayed with his older brother, Jacob, who had left Warsaw one year earlier, until he was finally able to obtain a visa in March 1940 for the United States. On arrival in New York, he stayed in Brooklyn with his oldest sister, Sarah, the only one of his sisters to escape Europe.

In fall 1940, Heschel began teaching at Hebrew Union College. Five difficult years ensued. He was not yet fluent in English, and his observance of Jewish dietary and ritual obligations set him apart from the customs of the Reformed institution. He took meals in his room since the cafeteria didn't keep kosher. He also found the American students much less prepared to handle Hebrew texts than those he had taught in Germany. Efforts to save his mother and three sisters in Poland failed, and they perished in the Holocaust. Years later in his inaugural lecture as a visiting professor at Union Theological Seminary in New York, he would epitomize the tragedy by introducing himself "as a person who was able to leave Warsaw, the city in which I was born, just six weeks before the disaster began. My destination was New York; it would have been Auschwitz or Treblinka. I am a brand plucked from the fire in which my people was burned to death. I am a brand plucked from the fire of an altar of Satan on which millions of human lives were exterminated to evil's greater glory."[9]

In 1945, Heschel met a young concert pianist, Sylvia Strauss, at a dinner party. They discovered that they shared mutual interests in music, philosophy, and art, and fell in love. In December 1946, they married and moved to New York City, where Heschel accepted a teaching position as a professor of Jewish mysticism and ethics at the Jewish Theological Seminary, the center of Conservative Judaism in the United States. Their only child, Susannah, was born in 1952.

From his small, overcrowded office at the Jewish Theological Seminary, a steady stream of books began to appear, including essays on the philosophy of religion from the perspective of the phenomenological analysis of religious experience; biographies of Jewish thinkers such as Moses Maimonides and Abravanel; the circle of followers of the Ba'al Shem Tov; an elegiac depiction of the Eastern European Hasidic culture destroyed by the Shoah; and theological reflections on the Sabbath, the relationship of human beings and God, and a masterful revision in English translation of his dissertation on the consciousness of the prophets. As Susannah Heschel noted, "One looks hard to find discussion of [direct] political activism in my father's scholarly and theological writing of the 1940s and '50s. As he later explained in an interview, it was revising his dissertation on the prophets for publication in English during the early 1960s that convinced him that he must be involved in human affairs, in human suffering."[10]

In *The Prophets*, Heschel offered his clearest articulation of the connection between religion and politics, sanctity and social activism. The relationship between God and human beings is not only that of creator to creature but also one of mutual partnership. He made this radical claim: "God is in need of human beings." We all see the cruelty of humans and the misery they cause, but strive to stifle our conscience by cultivating indifference. Note that Heschel does not exempt himself from blame but speaks of "we," including himself among the ranks of those Thomas Merton would call "guilty bystanders." As Heschel would famously put it, "Few are guilty but all are responsible." It is the divinely imposed task of the prophet to break down the wall of our indifference by voicing the suffering and anguish of the poor, the widow, the orphan, and the oppressed of our society.[11]

To the prophet ... God does not reveal himself in an abstract absoluteness, but in a personal and intimate relation to the world. He does not simply command and expect obedience; He is also moved and affected by what happens in the world, and reacts accordingly. Events and human actions arouse in Him joy or sorrow, pleasure or wrath. He is not conceived as judging the world in detachment. He reacts in an intimate and subjective manner, and thus determines the value of events. Quite obviously in the biblical view, man's deeds may move Him, affect Him, grieve Him or, on the other hand, gladden and please Him. This notion that God can be intimately affected, that He possesses not merely intelligence and will, but also pathos, basically defines the prophetic consciousness of God.

Unlike the unmoved mover of the philosophers,

unknown and indifferent to man ... the God of Israel is a God Who loves, a God Who is known to, and concerned with, man. He not only rules the world in the majesty of His might and wisdom, but reacts intimately to the events of history. He does not judge men's deeds impassively and with aloofness; His judgment is imbued with the attitude of One to Whom those actions are of the most intimate and profound concern. God does not stand outside the range of human suffering and sorrow. He is personally involved in, even stirred by, the conduct and fate of man. Pathos denotes, not an idea of goodness, but a living care; not an immutable example, but an act or attitude composed of various spiritual elements; no mere contemplative survey of the world, but a passionate summons.[12]

Heschel links God's pathos for humanity to the biblical idea of man as created in the image and likeness of God. "Man is not only an image of God; he is a perpetual concern of God. The idea of pathos adds a new dimension to human existence. Whatever man does affects not only his own life, but also the life of God insofar as it is directed to man. The import of man raises him beyond the level of mere creature. He is a consort, a partner, a factor in the life of God."[13] Thus, "the gulf that separates man from God is transcended by His pathos." The prophet then "suffers in himself harms done to others, whose greatest passion is compassion, whose greatest strength is love and defiance of despair." Love and defiance of despair are the prime contribution of the prophet to human understanding of God's involvement in history.

Heschel's own internal integration of his analysis of the prophetic role was revealed in his choice of extra-biblical exemplars. He customarily observed the anniversary of the death of Albert Schweitzer, in his classes at the Jewish Theological Seminary. He spoke of how Schweitzer forsook glory as a famed philosopher, organist, and musicologist to become a common doctor in a clinic in a remote area of Africa to atone for the sins of the white race. And in the last chapter of his book on Maimonides, Heschel proposed that the reason the famous philosopher abandoned his unfinished scholarly work in order to heal the sick, was because he decided to move from contemplation to action on behalf of suffering humanity. Maimonides came to realize that contemplation of God and service to man are one. "In contrast to his earlier view that man's ultimate perfection is purely intellectual . . . he now defines man's ultimate end as *the imitation of God's ways* and actions, namely kindness, justice, righteousness."[14]

Robert McAfee Brown, who as a faculty member at Union Theological Seminary (and founding member, with Heschel, of Clergy and Laymen Concerned about Vietnam) got to know Heschel well, perceptively described the social implications of Heschel's vision of sharing the divine pathos:

God needs us: the fulfillment of the divine intention for the world cannot be accomplished apart from the work of God's children. . . . God has placed us here in the midst of an unfinished creation, and has given us the task of helping to bring it to fulfillment. That is why we were created. That is the purpose of our lives. That is the content of our prayer. That is why our deeds and our prayers can never be separated. That is why intention and deed are both necessary. That is why there must be both *kavanah*, the right intention, and *mitzvah*, the actual deed. And here . . . we see how the outer and the inner come together for Heschel. For just as the contemplation about God leads to the doing of deeds so the doing of deeds is one of the "starting points of contemplation about God."

And foreshadowing the cry of later liberation theology: "The prophets have a bias in favor of the poor."[15]

In January 1963, the National Conference of Christians and Jews organized a conference in Chicago on the topic of religion and race timed to coincide with the centenary of the Emancipation Proclamation. Heschel was invited to deliver the opening address—an address that ranks among the most perceptive and eloquent to come out of the civil rights movement. Divided into five sections, his speech used poetic and aphoristic phrases, reminiscent of the biblical book of Proverbs, to apply the moral insights of the Bible, Talmud, Hasidic tradition, and Kabbalistic mysticism to the issue of racism and the struggle for civil rights.

Heschel started by wryly describing "the first" conference on religion and race, as the dialogue between Moses and the pharaoh. Moses declared: "Thus says the Lord, the God of Israel, let My people go that they may celebrate a feast to Me." And the pharaoh retorted: "Who is the Lord that I should heed this voice and let Israel go? I do not know the Lord, and moreover I will not let Israel go." While this beginning probably aroused some surprised chuckles in the audience, the more perceptive would have recognized Heschel's allusion to the fundamental contradiction between two mythical American identities—that of those who saw the nation as a "New Israel," freed from the bondage of the Old World and at ease in the Promised Land of milk and honey, and that of those black Americans who experienced the United States as the old Egypt in which they still toiled in bondage. They were still singing "Go Down Moses and Tell Ol' Pharaoh to Let My People Go!" Then he made the allusion plain: the Exodus began long ago, but is far from complete. "In fact, it was easier for the children of Israel to cross the Red Sea than for a Negro to cross certain university campuses." In one bold rhetorical stroke, Heschel reversed the celebratory myth of American exceptionalism and embraced the ongoing struggle for black liberation in the civil rights movement as the present-day instantiation of Exodus—a rhetorical strategy honed by generations of African American preachers and orators, stretching back to the days of slavery.

He then proceeded to question the validity of the conference title, Religion *and* Race, by erasing the "and." Religion and race are inherently contradictory. How can the two be uttered together? "To act in the spirit of religion is to unite what lies apart, to remember that humanity as a whole is God's beloved child. To act in the spirit of race is to sunder, to slash, to dismember the flesh of living humanity. . . . How can we hear the word 'race' and feel no self-reproach? As a standard of values and behavior, race operates as a comprehensive doctrine, as racism. And racism is worse than idolatry. *Racism is satanism*, unmitigated evil." When he spoke these words, it is likely that the analogy to the Holocaust with its "altars to Satan on which millions of human lives were exterminated to evil's greater glory," came to mind.

Like Ralph Ellison's protagonist in the novel *Invisible Man* (1952), Heschel diagnosed racism as an "eye disease" affecting the inner eyes with which one looks out on others, resulting in an inability to see the image of God in every person, which in effect is to see it in none. "To efface the divine image in another is to that extent to efface it in oneself," as Martin Luther King Jr. would similarly claim. Moreover, the rampant segregation of black people in the blighted urban ghettos is precisely an attempt to keep them "out of sight" and thus make it impossible to regard them as neighbors. Hence, "the hysteria that results when a Negro moves into our neighborhood." Segregation keeps them out of sight and out of mind, blinding our consciences and leading to indifference in our society more insidious than the evil itself. Even worse, the clergy has abdicated its prophetic role by insisting that ministers stay clear of civil rights protests lest they be seen as meddling in social problems. On the contrary, if it is people's task to complete God's design for human history, it is not enough to merely sit in pews. It is not enough to appeal to the government. We must welcome blacks and delight in enabling them to enjoy their rights. Interpersonal contact is crucial: "Equality means more than legal equality. It means personal involvement, fellowship, mutual resources and concern." It is time, Heschel urged, to take action, to make personal sacrifices, to repent. In fact, we should see the race issue as "God's gift to America, a spiritual opportunity to rise above complacent prosperity."[16]

Modeling personal concern, Heschel confessed, "My heart is sick when I think of the anguish and the sighs, of the quiet tears shed in the nights in the overcrowded dwellings in the slums of our great cities, of the pangs of despair, of the cup of humiliation that is running over." Heschel also proved himself to be a sensitive interpreter of the inner effects of racism, demonstrating his "sharing in the divine pathos for human suffering."[17] He placed an unusually strong emphasis on the damaging effects of racial discrimination as a form of public shaming. "How long will *I* continue to be tolerant of, even a participant in, acts of embarrassing and humiliating human beings, in restaurants, hotels, buses, or parks, employment agencies, public schools and universities? One ought to rather be shamed than put others to shame." Heschel even equated shaming with murder, describing it as a form of soul murder, which is even worse than physical murder and a more heinous offense against the commandments of God.[18]

He presciently warned against two forms of moral apathy: that caused by indifference, and that caused by despair at the difficulty of effecting major social and attitudinal change in deeply ingrained and institutionalized racist attitudes and behaviors. Racism is an evil of tremendous power, but God's will transcends all powers. Surrender to despair is surrender to evil. It is important to feel anxiety; it is sinful to wallow in despair. Heschel admonished that "this world, this society can be redeemed. God has a stake in our moral predicament. I cannot believe that God will be defeated."[19]

In a powerful panegyric, he praised "the Spirituality of Negroes, their attachment to the Bible," and asserted, "Their power of worship may prove to be a blessing to all mankind." And he concluded his address with the words from the prophet Amos (5:24, but his unique translation) that King would frequently recite as a refrain and would eventually be carved on the Civil Rights Memorial in Montgomery, Alabama: "Let justice roll down like waters / and righteousness like a mighty stream." For Heschel, this verse expressed his own prophetic consciousness that the movement for justice is a powerful force charged with the omnipotence of God.[20]

At the Chicago conference Heschel first met King, who delivered the keynote address. The two became friends as well as colleagues. When Heschel joined the Selma march in 1965, the organizers were well aware of his book *The Prophets*, and the iconic power of his presence positioned Heschel as one of the leaders in the front row of marchers, standing side by side with King, Ralph Bunche, and Ralph Abernathy. Susannah Heschel revealed that

> in an unpublished memoir he wrote upon returning from Selma, my father describes the extreme hostility he encountered from whites in Alabama, from the moment he arrived at the airport, and the kindness he was shown by Dr. King's assistants, particularly the Reverend Andrew Young, who watched over him during the march with great concern. Just before the march began, a service was held in a small chapel [Brown Chapel AME Church] where my father read Psalm 27, "The Lord is my light and my salvation; whom shall I fear?" And Dr. King gave a sermon describing three typologies among the children of Israel in the wilderness. . . . For my father the march was a religious moment. He wrote in his memoir: "I thought of my having walked with Hasidic rabbis on various occasions. I felt a sense of the Holy in what I was doing. Dr. King expressed several times to me his appreciation. He said, 'I cannot tell you how much your presence means to us. You cannot imagine how often Reverend Vivian and I speak about you.' Dr. King said to me that this was the greatest day in his life and the most important civil-rights demonstration."[21]

Heschel publicly expressed his close affinity with King at a celebration of Heschel's sixtieth birthday during the annual assembly of Conservative Jewish Rabbis, on March 25, 1968, ten days before King's assassination.[22] After the assembled rabbis paid tribute to King by singing a moving version of "We Shall Overcome" in Hebrew, Heschel introduced him:

> Where does moral religious leadership in America come from today? The politicians are astute, the establishment is proud, and the market place is busy. Placid, happy, merry, the people pursue their work, enjoy their leisure, and life is fair. People buy, sell, celebrate, and rejoice. They fail to realize that in the midst of our affluent cities there are districts of despair, areas of distress. Where does God dwell in America today? Is He at home with those who are complacent, indifferent to other people's agony, devoid of mercy? Is He not rather with the poor and the contrite in the slums? Dark is the world for me, for all its cities and stars. If not for the few signs of God's radiance, who could stand such agony, such darkness? Where in America today do we hear a voice like the voice of the prophets of Israel? Martin Luther King is a sign that God has not forsaken the United States of America. God has sent him to us. His presence is the hope of America. His mission is sacred, his leadership of supreme importance to every one of us. The situation of the poor in America is our plight, our sickness. To be deaf to their cry is to condemn ourselves. Martin Luther King is a voice, a vision, and a way. I call upon every Jew to harken to his voice, to share his vision, to follow in his way. The whole future of America will depend upon the impact and influence of Dr. King. May everyone present give of his strength to this great spiritual leader, Martin Luther King.[23]

Heschel invited King and his family to join his family for the Passover seder on April 16, 1968. The invitation read, "The ritual and the celebration of that evening seek to make present to us the spirit and the wonder of the exodus from Egypt. It is my feeling that your participation at a Seder celebration would be of very great significance." King was assassinated on April 4. Susannah Heschel noted the reaction: "My father came home from the office early. He heard the news and got into bed and turned out the lights. He never just stayed in bed, but that day and night he did."[24] Coretta Scott King invited Heschel to speak at King's funeral. At the afternoon Morehouse service that followed the morning service at Ebenezer Baptist Church, Heschel chose the suffering servant passage from Isaiah—a passage that Jews applied to the people Israel and Christians to Jesus:

> He was despised and rejected by men;
> a man of sorrows, and acquainted with grief:
> and as one from whom men hid their faces
> He was despised, and we esteemed him not.
>
> —Isaiah 53:3

Describing the correspondences between the theologies of Heschel and King, Susannah Heschel noted that both men shared in their speeches the primacy of the Exodus motif. And Heschel's concept of divine pathos, a category central to his theology, is mirrored in King's understanding of the nature of God's involvement with humanity. For both, the theological was intimately intertwined with the political, and that conviction provided the basis of the spiritual affinity they felt for each other.[25]

As the civil rights struggle brought Heschel together with the Baptist King, interfaith dialogue brought him into a surprising alliance with the Roman Catholic monk Thomas Merton. Pope John XXIII in calling the Second Vatican Council decided the council ought to make a statement on the relationship of the church to Judaism and asked the Austrian cardinal Augustine Bea, chair of the secretariat dealing with non-Christian religions, to manage the process. Heschel acted as a liaison on behalf of the American Jewish Committee to draft suggestions for the statement, stressing the need for the council to reject the age-old charge of deicide against the Jews for the crucifixion of Jesus as well as rescinding the church's insistence on the conversion of the Jews to Christianity, and for the Catholic Church to express repentance for its history of anti-Semitic persecution. An initial draft reflected these suggestions in clear and powerful language, but ran into objections in conciliar debates from bishops in Muslim countries worried about its political ramifications. Rumors reported in the press indicated that a revised draft under consideration would weaken the language of the first. Alarmed, Heschel and the American Jewish Committee urgently complained to Cardinal Bea, and Heschel turned for help to the Trappist monk Merton, with whom he had struck up a friendly correspondence.

Merton had been reading Heschel and wrote to him with admiration for *God in Search of Man*, which he had used in the class for novices he taught at the Abbey of Gethsemane. On October 23, 1960, Heschel replied:

> Dear Father Merton: Your kind letter came as a precious affirmation of what I have known for a long time: of how much there is we share in the ways of trying to sense what is given in the Word, in the things created, in the moments He continues to create, in the effort to counteract the desecration of stillness. For many good hours in reading some of your writings, I am indebted to you. . . . I am sending you some books of mine. At the moment I am trying to complete a book on the prophets—a humiliating undertaking. . . . I cherish your

statement: "How absurd it is . . . to attach such overweening importance to our reflections and so little to the revelation itself." And still reflecting we must, only that all reflection fades when we get close to the light.[26]

On October 29, in his journal, Merton noted the reception of Heschel's letter: "Abraham Heschel wrote an amiable and humble letter and sent three books. I am happy and consoled. He is the most significant spiritual (religious) writer in this country at the moment. I like his depth and his realism. He knows God! Is writing now on the prophets, and is worthy to do it."[27] Further correspondence between them focused on the Vatican II declaration on relations to the Jews in the document that became *Nostra Aetate*. Heschel, distraught by what was happening on the "Jewish statement," visited Merton at Gethsemani on July 13, 1964. The prior, Father Flavian Flood, invited Merton to accompany him on the drive to the Louisville airport to pick up Heschel. As he remembered the encounter, the two were soon joking and laughing in the car on the way back to the abbey. Presented with a steak dinner (an exception to the meatless monastic diet), Heschel demurred because it was not kosher. He and the monks enjoyed chatting until late in the evening, even though they had to rise at 2:00 a.m. to chant the morning office. The next day, Heschel expressed his concern to Merton that the original draft was being watered down due to pressure from bishops in Muslim countries, worried that the statement might be construed as favorable to the state of Israel. He feared that this opposition had weakened Cardinal Bea's influence. Merton expressed confidence in Bea's intentions and diplomatic skill, and promised to write him a letter, which he did the next day, July 14, a copy of which he mailed to Heschel on July 27.

In his letter to Cardinal Bea, Merton commented that he and his fellow monks were praying "that God may see fit to grant his Church the very great favor and grace of understanding the true meaning of this opportunity for repentance and truth which is being offered her." Merton revealed his views on the controversy in a journal entry dated July 1964, around the time of Heschel's visit. "[The Jews] remain the people of God, since His promises are not made void nor are they being transferred en bloc to the Church without further ado, the Jews . . . are still the object of his special mercy and concern, a sign of his concern." In the end, the final version restored most of the ideas that Heschel had favored, although it still lacked the forcefulness of the earlier draft. At the fourth session of the council, the bishops approved it by a vote of 2,221 to 88.[28] Pope Paul VI immediately proclaimed the document as church doctrine.

In addition to civil rights and ecumenical relations, Heschel was moved to active protest by America's military involvement in Southeast Asia. The continued escalation of the bombing of Vietnam profoundly disturbed him. In January 1966, he helped to form Clergy and Laymen (later changed to Laity) Concerned about the War in Vietnam. On January 31, the organization sponsored a demonstration against the war in Washington, DC. At the prayer meeting, Heschel offered the following meditation on the words of the prophet Ezekiel (34:25–31):

> The encounter of man and God is an encounter within the world. We meet within a situation of shared suffering, of shared responsibility. This is implied in believing in One God in whose eyes there is no dichotomy of here and there, of me and them. They and I are one; here is there, and there is here. What goes on over there happens even

here. Oceans divide us, God's presence unites us, and God is present wherever man is afflicted, and all of humanity is embroiled in every agony wherever it may be. Though not a native of Vietnam, ignorant of its language and traditions, I am involved in the plight of the Vietnamese. To be human means not to be immune to other people's suffering. People in Vietnam, North and South, have suffered, and all of us are hurt.[29]

In his introduction of King at Riverside Church on April 4, 1967, the occasion when King publicly announced his opposition to the Vietnam War, Heschel took the opportunity to clearly state his own justification for condemning the US prosecution of an illegitimate war:

The state requires that the citizen risk his life for it; the acceptance of sacrifice is one of our essential duties, but it is also the duty of the citizen, who, after careful study, becomes convinced that a war his country is involved in is both morally wrong and politically absurd, to do his utmost to stop it. . . . Our thoughts on Vietnam are sores, destroying our trust, ruining our most cherished commitments with burdens of shame. We are pierced to the core with pain, and it is our duty as citizens to say no to the subversiveness of our government, which is ruining the values we cherish. . . . The blood we shed in Vietnam makes a mockery of all our proclamations, dedications, celebrations. Has our conscience become a fossil, is all mercy gone? . . . We are here because our own integrity as human beings is decaying in the agony and merciless killing done in our name. In a free society, some are guilty and all are responsible. We are here to call upon the governments of the United States as well as North Vietnam to stand still and to consider that no victory is worth the price of terror. . . . Remember that the blood of the innocent cries forever. Should that blood stop to cry, humanity would cease to be.[30]

The radicalism of Heschel's political positions offended some of his colleagues at the Jewish Theological Seminary as well as others in the Jewish community. McAfee Brown reported that

> as he attempted to look at the world from a prophetic stance —in that daring notion of his that the prophet does not interpret God to the world but looks at the world through God's eyes—he was forced to take positions that many of his contemporaries thought demented and wrong and "mad." On no issue, perhaps, was this truer than on Vietnam. And his minority status was nowhere more evident than within the Jewish community itself, which did not appreciate Heschel's challenging the calculations of the Johnson administration, an administration that on more than one occasion sent emissaries to others in the Jewish community to say, none too gently, that unless Heschel cooled it, the Johnson administration might just diminish its military support to the State of Israel.[31]

Heschel's involvement in the antiwar movement brought him into association and close friendship with William Sloan Coffin, an outspoken activist and Yale University chaplain, and the Roman Catholic priests Philip and Daniel Berrigan, who both spent time in jail for their highly publicized acts of antiwar protest. Undoubtedly his support for such "radical" protesters disturbed some of his colleagues in the academy and rabbinate.

His daughter confirmed the unpopularity of Heschel's political stances: "Of course, my father's involvement in social issues did not always bring him the support of the Jewish community.

On the contrary, he was often fiercely opposed for the positions he took. It hurt to read articles in the local Jewish newspapers attacking him. Years later, many in the Jewish community who had opposed my father learned to take pride in the famous photographs showing him marching in the front lines in demonstrations with Martin Luther King, Jr."[32]

For many, Jews and Gentiles, the connection between Heschel's mysticism and his ethics—a connection foundational for his activism—remained opaque. The theological roots of his activism lay precisely in his mysticism. For Heschel, the Bible reveals God to be intimately involved in human history generally, and in the lives and deeds of individual persons specifically. Human actions, as the prophets reveal, have an effect on God. Moreover, Heschel's background in Hasidic mysticism and Kabbalah stressed that evil acts trap the sparks of divinity scattered throughout the universe. It is our good deeds that free the divine sparks and help to restore God's redemptive presence in the world. In short, our actions hasten or delay the healing of the world. That is why marching in Selma was simultaneously a political act and an act of devotion helping to release the divine sparks into a world darkened by the evil of racism.

Perhaps Heschel's own clearest statement about the relationship between religion and political action is "On Prayer" from *Moral Grandeur and Spiritual Audacity*:

> Religion as an establishment must remain separated from the government. Yet prayer as a voice of mercy, as a cry for justice, as a plea for gentleness, must not be kept apart. Let the spirit of prayer dominate the world. Let the spirit of prayer interfere in the affairs of man. Prayer is private, a service of the heart: but let concern and compassion, born out of prayer, dominate public life. . . . There is a pressing urgency

to the work of justice and compassion. As long as there is a shred of hatred in a human heart, as long as there is a vacuum without compassion anywhere in the world, there is an emergency.

Taking stock of the depth of evil in the twentieth century, Heschel lamented:

The malignity of our situation is increasing rapidly; the magnitude of evil is spreading furiously, surpassing our ability to be shocked. The human soul is too limited to experience dismay in proportion to what has happened in Auschwitz, in Hiroshima. . . . It is with shame and anguish that I recall that it was possible for a Roman Catholic church adjoining the extermination camp in Auschwitz to offer communion to the officers of the camp, to people who day after day drove thousands of people to be killed in the gas chambers. Let there be an end to the separation of church and God, of sacrament and callousness, of religion and justice, of prayer and compassion. . . . Prayer is meaningless unless it is subversive, unless it seeks to overthrow and to ruin the pyramids of callousness, hatred, opportunism, falsehoods. . . . The world is aflame with evil and atrocity, the scandal of perpetual desecration of the world cries to high heaven. And we, coming face to face with it, are either involved as callous participants or, at best remain indifferent onlookers. The relentless pursuit of our interests makes us oblivious of reality itself. Nothing we experience has value in itself; nothing counts unless it can be turned to our advantage, into a means for serving our self-interests.[33]

Rabbi Heschel died in his sleep on the Sabbath, December 23, 1972. In Jewish tradition, a peaceful death in one's sleep is considered a sign of great piety, and to die on the Sabbath is to die "with a kiss" from God. In a television interview conducted only ten days before his death, Heschel briefly summed up the trajectory of his life: "Early in my life, my great love was for learning, studying. And the place where I preferred to live was my study and books and writing and thinking. I've learned from the prophets that I have to be involved in the affairs of man, in the affairs of suffering man."[34]

Figure 2.1 A. J. Muste. Courtesy of the Joint Archives of Holland.

CHAPTER 2

A. J. MUSTE

THE REDEMPTIVE POWER OF NONVIOLENT SUFFERING

> Thus it is that whenever love that will suffer unto
> death is manifested, whenever a true Crucifixion takes
> place, unconquerable power is released into the stream
> of history. The intuition that says that God has been
> let loose on the earth when such devotion is mani-
> fested is absolutely sound.
>
> —A. J. Muste, *Essays*

So wrote Muste, the director of the pacifist organization the Fellowship of Reconciliation (FOR), in 1943, in
"What the Bible Teaches about Freedom." In this sermonic
essay addressed "To the Negro Church," he predicted the
cost that black Americans and their white allies would have
to pay to end segregation in the United States.[1] Published by
the FOR as a pamphlet, the essay was distributed widely to
black churches and among members of the March on Washington movement planned by A. Phillip Randolph. According to Muste, the core of the nonviolent movement for social
change is the willingness of the activist to suffer, even to die,
to achieve a more just society. This belief, radical as it may
seem, served as the lodestar for his long life of activism in the
causes of peace, labor, civil rights, and nuclear disarmament.

Abraham Johannes Muste, the oldest of five children, was born in Zierikzee, a small town in the Netherlands on January 8, 1885, to Martin and Adriana (Zonker) Muste. His father was a coachman in the employ of a minor noble. Muste's family was poor, living in one room, surrounded by sleeping alcoves. He "retained vivid memories of his first six years . . . moments when, as a four or five year old, he was shaken by sensations of beauty, awe, horror, and 'a sort of revelation' about the otherness and yet the loveliness of fellow human beings."[2] His mother's four brothers had immigrated to the United States, settling in Grand Rapids, Michigan, where they had established small businesses in the large Dutch émigré community. Her brothers reported that economic opportunities were much better there, and offered to give her and her family financial support for ship fare. Convinced, the Mustes sailed in 1901, settled in the cramped quarters of steerage. En route, Adriana Muste fell sick and on arrival at Castle Garden (New York's port of entry before Ellis Island), their entry was delayed while she recuperated. There a friendly hospital attendant insisted on calling the six-year-old Muste "Abraham Lincoln." Years later, he recalled that he had never heard of Lincoln then, but "passing my youth in Michigan not far from Springfield in the 1890s, when the Middle West in its own imagination and feeling, still lived in the days of John Brown, the Emancipation Proclamation, the martyred President—all this is part of my inmost being."[3]

The adult Muste would define for himself the significance of the biblical figure he was really named for. Abraham too had left his native land—Ur of the Chaldees, in obedience to the command of God, whose voice he followed wherever it led on the winding journey toward the land promised to him and his descendants. The fidelity of the patriarch Abraham to the path willed by God, with all its twists and turns, seemed to Muste an apt map of meaning for his own life's journey. In one of a series of "autobiographical sketches" he wrote for the radical journal *Liberation* in the late 1950s, Muste reflected on this eponymous connection in terms that are remarkably similar to Heschel's. He asserted that in the biblical concept of history epitomized by Abraham, God works in people's daily lives, offering us the opportunity to become coworkers and cocreators with God in moving toward a goal. The movement of people in space and time models God's design, which is not static but instead draws us ever onward, toward the goal of establishing a society of peace and justice. The experience of emigration-immigration, so characteristic of American identity, becomes the symbol of obedience to God's will.[4]

Raised in the Dutch Reformed Church, Muste recalled that the solemnity of the Sunday services he experienced at the age of six or seven "gave me a feeling of having entered another world, the 'real' world." He singled out especially "the experience of the Good Friday and the Easter services of his thirteenth year as 'something that could be called mystical.' On the afternoon of that particular Easter Sunday, as he was walking out of doors by himself . . . suddenly 'the world took on a new brightness' and 'Christ is risen indeed' was spoken within him. 'From that day,' he later maintained, 'God was real to me.'"[5] This was the first of several mystical experiences that would validate critical decisions later in his adult life. Shortly after this adolescent vision, the consistory of the church accepted him as a full member, though customarily confirmation was not granted until the age of seventeen or eighteen. As an adult, mystical experience would confirm Muste's faith during periods when doubt about traditional doctrine and disappointment over ecclesiastical complicity with the status quo shook his commitment to Christianity.

Muste's parents enrolled him in a church-affiliated grammar school, whose headmaster was his mother's nephew, but they soon transferred him to a public school with a more varied curriculum and less heavy-handed discipline. There he became an avid reader, "with a book always in hand," according to his brother. In eighth grade, an essay Muste wrote on child labor won first place in a writing contest. The first prize, a package of books, included Ralph Waldo Emerson's *Essays*, "which was," Muste recalled, "the most seminal influence of all on my thinking. With Lincoln, Emerson was a creator of that 'American Dream,' which, along with the great passages of the Hebrew-Christian Scriptures, molded and nourished my mind and spirit." After grade school, he was admitted to Hope College Preparatory School in Holland, Michigan, in September 1898, at the precocious age of thirteen, the youngest student in the school. In 1902, he entered Hope College as a sophomore and completed the four-year curriculum in three. Muste participated in sports in both prep school and college, including basketball (as captain of the state champion team) and baseball (a lifelong passion).[6]

Graduating from Hope in 1905, at the age of twenty, he took a year off to teach Greek and English in a classical academy in Iowa. A major factor in his decision was the opportunity to court a girl he had fallen in love with during his senior year at Hope, Anna Huizinga, who lived near the academy. They became engaged but decided to wait on marriage until he had completed his studies for the ministry. In September 1906, Muste enrolled at the New Brunswick Theological Seminary of the Dutch Reformed Church in New Jersey. To supplement what he judged to be a mediocre academic program, he took graduate courses in philosophy, first at New York University, and later at Columbia University, where he first saw John Dewey (who later became a devoted friend) and occasionally heard William James lecture. In 1909, he graduated from the New Brunswick Seminary and was duly licensed to preach by the classis of the Fourth Reformed Church in Grand Rapids. He married Huizinga at her home on June 21, 1909 (a marriage that would last until Anna's death forty-five years later) and was installed at the end of June as the first minister of the Fort Washington Collegiate Church, built in New York in 1909, to pastor people moving into upper Manhattan. An attractive bonus for Muste was the location of the New York Yankee ballpark a few blocks from the church. And Union Theological Seminary was close enough for him to take courses. There the faculty member who especially influenced his theological views was Arthur Cushman McGiffert Sr., whose lectures on the history of Christian dogma were far and away the most brilliant that Muste had ever experienced. They opened up to him a new approach to the study of religion and new historical vistas, eventually forcing him into a reappraisal of the beliefs in which he had been raised. In a seminar at Union Theological Seminary, he first encountered a young Presbyterian minister named Norman Thomas, a fitting harbinger of the drastic change in politics that accompanied the radical revisions in his theology. As Muste vividly recalled years later in *Liberation*,

> The Republicanism in which I had been brought up also received rude shocks from the contacts of that period. These were the years of mushrooming sweatshops, of the terrible Triangle Fire in a garment factory, of the strikes which marked the founding of the garment trades unions, and, in Paterson [New Jersey] and more distant places, of the turbulent I.W.W. [Industrial Workers of the World] organizational campaigns and strikes. I had spent the summer of 1908 . . . as supply preacher at the Middle Collegiate Church on Second

Avenue and Seventh Street, in the very heart of the East Side. For the first time in my life I had really seen, and lived in, slums. I had walked the streets and parks on hot summer days and during the only slightly less oppressive evenings. I had climbed flights of stairs to call on sick and aged parishioners. Sometimes I had been barely able to endure the fetid smells and unceasing raucous noises. This was a very different poverty from that [I had experienced before]. As a result, I read some radical literature and was sympathetically disposed toward the workers in their desperate struggles.[7]

In 1912, he earned a second bachelor of divinity degree, magna cum laude, at Union Theological Seminary. There he claimed the prophets "really [came] alive for me." He began to see them as "fellows who preached politics, got into the actual struggle and cursed those who were grinding the faces of the poor." At the seminary, Muste was also introduced to the work of Walter Rauschenbusch and started to sympathize with Rauschenbusch's Social Gospel. But he did not immediately take personal action because of his preoccupation with the doubts about Christian doctrine that increasingly troubled him. Though supported by many in his congregation, Muste seriously began to consider leaving the ministry since he felt that he could no longer tell people he believed in the virgin birth or literal inspiration of scripture when he didn't. For a while it seemed impossible to hold on to any religious faith at all. He turned to McGiffert for council, and was advised to leave the pulpit and try "religious journalism or something of that sort."

Deeply troubled by this crisis of faith, he sought relief in nature. As described by Leilah Danielson in her definitive biography of Muste, "In early 1914 he and Anne left the city for the Catskills to reflect and recuperate. There he had a tremendous mystical experience that reassured him of God's existence and of God's love: 'I have now arrived at a perfect religious certainty, a peace of mind after a long period of doubt,' Muste proclaimed upon returning to the city."[8] In November of that year, he resigned from the Fort Washington Church and accepted an invitation to pastor the Central Congregational Church in Newtonville, Massachusetts. He reported another religious experience later on that confirmed the correctness of this decision. By this account, Anna and he were staying briefly in a hotel in New Jersey before taking up residence in Newtonville. She was recovering from an illness (or perhaps a miscarriage). He was apparently settled with his decision, when

> "I was walking late one morning down the corridor of the hotel.... Suddenly came again that experience of a great light flooding in upon the world making things stand forth 'in sunny outline brave and clear' and of God being truly present and all-sufficient." ... From the encounter came assurance, he later said, "that I had not the same Gospel as ever to preach but a much greater Gospel, in the sense that my understanding of it was enriched and my personal hold on God firmer." When he told Anna of his mystical insight, they both rejoiced and shared "a deep sense of ... the ultimate rightness of things."[9]

The doubt was gone.

Muste's relationship with his new, more doctrinally liberal congregation remained untroubled until the outbreak of World War I exposed an unexpected conflict over Muste's position on the morality of war. Muste himself alternated between supporting the war, on the one hand, and pacifism, on the other. It is worth quoting his own description of his life-changing commitment to pacifism because he reveals the principles behind his conversion, which he would defend for the rest of his life in disputes with those who denied that the Gospel of Jesus required pacifism:

> As recently as the late fall of 1914, war had not been a personal problem for me. Certainly in all the study of the Scriptures through which I had been led in that citadel of orthodoxy, New Brunswick, and in the hotbed of heresy which was Union—in those days—I had never been given an inkling that there might be such a thing as a pacifist interpretation of the Gospel. How then did it come about that, a year later, I found myself a convinced Christian pacifist? . . . The problem, as it presented itself to me, was simply one for the Christian conscience. . . . It was a problem which I could not evade because I had been brought up to take religion, specifically the Biblical teaching and Gospel ethic, seriously, and to abhor the sham which enables a person to preach what he does not try desperately to practice. Moreover, my upbringing had given me a definite attitude regarding the struggle which goes on perpetually in the human spirit and in society as to whether the Gospel demand shall be adjusted to the outward circumstances or the recalcitrant reality shall be made to conform to the high ethical demand. I did not believe that there is a pat rule which one can find in a proof text and apply to a complicated situation, thereby achieving perfection. I had received too solid a dose of Calvinism not to have a strong conviction about human frailty and corruption. It was this that had made me aware, long before Freud was more than a name to me, that when a man is sure that he is honest, he deceives himself; when he imagines himself to be pure, he is impure; and when we bask in the glow of the feeling that we love, the fact is that in subtle ways we hate. But this does not alter the nature of the demand the Gospel places upon us—or, if you prefer, the demand that is placed upon us because we belong to the family of man—that we be honest and pure and that

we love all men. The poet who does not agonize to translate the vision he sees truly and exactly into his poem is not a poet. The man who does not passionately strive to be honest, pure and loving is not a man. The temptation to pride and self-righteousness is real and pervasive. The temptation to adapt the Gospel's demand to circumstances and to abandon the hard effort to mold one's own life and the world according to that imperious demand is no less subtle and pervasive. As far as reading is concerned, what undoubtedly influenced me most, during the critical months of inner wrestling, to conclude that I could not "bend" the Sermon on the Mount and the whole concept of the Cross and suffering love to accommodate participation in war, was the serious reading of the Christian mystics. Among the important books on some of these mystics were those by Rufus M. Jones, a leading Quaker. Thus I came to know about Quakers of past and present, Quaker meetings, the Quaker "peace testimony." It was the first time that these things suggested anything to me other than the man on the Quaker Oats box. My wrestling with these matters resulted in my joining, early in 1916, the Fellowship of Reconciliation, which had been founded at Cambridge University in December, 1914, and established in this country in November of the following year. Thus I became publicly identified as a Christian pacifist.[10]

Reading the mystic Rufus Jones likely helped confirm Muste's movement away from the restrictions of ecclesiastical institutions with their stress on dogmatic definitions toward an emphasis on the centrality of personal religious experience —a common response to the corrosive power of modern scriptural and historical scholarship on literal interpretations of traditional faith claims. As Jones wrote in *The Social Law in the Spiritual World* (1904), "The mystic finds religion, not in the institutions which history describes, not in the creeds, which have been formulated to satisfy intellectual demands, not in organized form through which men give expression to their religious activities—he finds the heart of religion in his own consciousness of God."[11] Jones also insisted that religious experience ought to result in social action to transform the world into the kingdom of God—an ethical emphasis that resonated deeply with Muste's own sense of integrity. Jones contended that the contribution of the Society of Friends is its "serious attempt to unite inward, mystical religion with active, social endeavors, and to maintain a religious fellowship without a rigid ecclesiastical system, and with large scope for personal initiative, immediate revelation and individual responsibility"—goals that Muste came completely to share.[12] Moreover, William James, whose occasional lectures Muste had attended at Columbia, underscored the importance of appreciating experience in analyzing the psychological meaning of religion in his widely influential study *The Varieties of Religious Experience*, published in 1902.

Finally, Muste committed to pacifism and discovered to his sorrow that he was no longer able to comfort the grieving parishioners who lost sons in battle, including, poignantly, his next-door neighbors. In his resignation sermon on December 9, 1917, he declared that "Jesus was a pacifist and that the followers of Jesus could be nothing else. The real task of the church is to create the spiritual conditions that should stop the war and render all wars unthinkable." He added that his own dedication to that task had recently been sanctioned by "a mystical experience of God" that had come on the preceding day, "for the second time in my life," and left him "happy and at rest in God. The war no longer has me by the throat."[13]

In January 1918, he enrolled as minister to the Providence, Rhode Island, Society of Friends, with a home and small salary. Although he later renewed his clerical credentials within the Presbyterian Church, the Society of Friends with its combination of experiential piety and social service offered Muste spiritual sustenance for the rest of his life. In addition to the Society of Friends, Muste focused his attention on the formation of a loosely organized intentional community called the Comradeship. "Those of us identified with The Comradeship (consisting of a group of men and women formed out of the Boston members of the FOR) in late 1918 and early 1919 were wrestling with the question of how to organize our lives so that they would truly express the teachings and spirit of Jesus, or, in other terms, faith in the way of truth, nonviolence and love." The group considered forming a community on the land as well as one in the city to further the struggle against war, and for economic justice and racial equality in the competitive society of the United States. Nothing came of this idea due to Muste's total immersion in the sixteen-week-long Lawrence, Massachusetts, textile strike. While generally critical of monastic retreat and asceticism, he and another founding member of the FOR, Harold Rotzel, arose at about five o'clock every morning for several weeks. They read the New Testament (especially the Sermon on the Mount), analyzed the passages, meditated on each phrase, even each word, prayed, and asked themselves what obedience to those precepts meant for them in the here and now. They were thinking in terms of forming an "intentional community." Along with other members of the FOR and a number of Quakers, they did constitute a "fellowship of sharing and concern," in a substantial measure. During most of the period that they held the early morning sessions, strikes were not in their thoughts at all. In a psychological and spiritual sense, however, those hours of meditation and self-searching constituted ideal preparation for what they soon were to face in the nearby city of Lawrence shortly after the start of 1919.[14] In effect, they were practicing the ancient Christian spiritual exercise of *Lectio Divina* (spiritual or divine reading), meditation, prayer, and application in preparation for action—"contemplation in a world of action," as Thomas Merton would put it years later. Their community-centered program also bore remarkable resemblance to the ideals of the Catholic Worker movement founded in the 1930s.

The Lawrence textile strike, which began in February 1919, put to the test the Comradeship's commitment to social as well as personal change. Three members, including Muste, Rotzel, and Cedric Long, visited the strikers, and were asked to lead the strike committee because of their articulate speech and outside connections. Muste was also asked to become executive secretary of the strike committee and quickly found himself, at the age of thirty-four, leading a force of thirty thousand strikers from twenty or more different nationalities. He not only led marches and picket lines but also like the other strikers, endured beatings from the police and time in the Lawrence jail. At one point the strikers faced down machine guns. Muste resolutely insisted on nonviolence despite the provocations of the owners and police along with the demands of agent provocateurs that they should respond in kind. Years later, he acknowledged the vague influence of Mahatma Gandhi. At the time of the Lawrence strike in 1919, he was already interested in the techniques of nonviolent direct action as part of pacifism. He had heard of Gandhi in a general way, but hadn't studied Gandhi's methods yet. The strike was ultimately settled with the owners in May 1919.

Tempered by fire in labor struggles, Muste served as the general secretary of the newly formed Amalgamated Textile Workers of America. "The two and a quarter years that I served as general secretary of the A.T.W. were made up of week after week of unremitting, desperate effort to establish a beachhead . . . of unionism in a chaotic industry, during a period of social ferment, postwar economic crisis and anti-labor hysteria." He resigned in 1921 to become education director of the Brookwood Labor College fifty miles north of New York City. Twelve more years of labor involvement followed. "I can see in retrospect that in some of its aspects the labor education experiment at Brookwood was a spiritual child of The Comradeship."[15] In 1933, a rift occurred at the college that led to his departure.

The Brookwood Labor College conflict resulted from a struggle with the more conservative leadership of the American Federation of Labor, who found Muste in particular and Brookwood in general too radical in their criticism of the mainstream labor establishment. The federation leaders retaliated by accusing the school of being tainted with Communist influence, and recommended that all its unions withdraw financial support and cease sending students. Dewey believed that "the condemnation of Brookwood . . . is a part of the policy to eliminate from the labor movement the schools and influences that endeavor to develop independent leaders of organized labor who are interested in a less passive social policy than that now carried on by the American Federation of Labor." Ensuing factionalism and personal attacks brought out the worst in Muste. He succumbed to short-temperedness and intolerance in his personal relationships with those who opposed him. Moreover, he began to abandon his stance of pacifism in support of outright sympathy for labor's resort to violence.[16]

Against the backdrop of the chaos of the radical labor movement in the1930s, Muste helped establish the American Worker's Party in 1933, intended to be a "third way" between Communism and Socialism, only to see it taken over by the Trotskyites. Financial hard times for Muste and his family were alleviated by donations from friends and admirers, including those who disagreed with his revolutionary politics. Years later he explained the attraction of radical politics for him: "It was on the Left—and here . . . the Communists cannot be excluded—that one found people who were truly '*religious*' in the sense that they were virtually completely committed, they were betting their lives on the cause they embraced. Often they gave up ordinary comforts, security, life itself, with a burning devotion which few Christians display toward the Christ whom they profess as Lord and incarnation of God."[17]

In 1936, Muste and Anna made a fateful trip to Europe to meet personally with Leon Trotsky in Norway as well as other Trotskyite leaders gathered from several countries in Paris, and recover from the strains and stresses of the all-consuming labor struggles that left them both exhausted. After the Trotskyite meetings, he and Anna followed a restful schedule of tourism and sightseeing in Switzerland and Paris. While walking alone one day, Muste entered the old church of Saint-Sulpice. What happened next changed Muste's life forever:

> Casually, one afternoon, I walked into [Saint-Sulpice]. It was being repaired. There was a certain impression of solidity about it, but it had too many statues of saints for my taste. I sat down on a bench near the front and looked at the cross. Without the slightest premonition of what was going to happen, I was saying to myself: "This is where you belong"; and "belong" again, in spirit, to the Church of Christ I did from that moment on. I felt as if the hand of God had drawn me up out of those "titanic glooms of chasmed fears" of which Francis Thompson sings and had catapulted me back into the Church. Even as these events were passing before me, I was saying to myself: "You see how it is. What you have all along been seeking is what the Marxist calls 'The Party' and what the religious man calls the 'True Church' and that is indeed

the crucial question of our day: what is the instrument by which the revolution is to be achieved, the Kingdom of God established? We cannot go on as we are. The great deliverance must come. But how? Where is The Party? Where is the True Church? I could not rest without an answer."[18]

The building was under repair; scaffolding detracted from the altar, and the whole church seemed much cluttered with statues. Yet when Muste stepped into the sanctuary, these distractions receded, and a "deep and singing peace" came over him. Physically he heard and saw nothing unusual. But inwardly, he experienced what must have been meant by the biblical description of the time "when the morning stars sang together" (Job 38:7). A symbolic interpretation of Muste's experience would notice that he took a seat facing the altar and cross, both of which had been restored in 1802, when the secularized "Temple of Victory" was reconsecrated for Christian worship after its desecration in 1793 by the French revolutionary regime. As he looked on the symbols of the crucified and resurrected Christ, an inner voice said, "This is where you belong, in the church, not outside it." It seems that the church acted as an "objective correlative" of his subjective experience—that is, his own reconversion from revolutionary dedication to Christian identity. He immediately determined that he must break with the Trotskyite movement and rededicate his life to the church. "This is where you belong, and belong again, in spirit, to the Church of Christ I did from that moment on." Muste, the secularized revolutionary, emerged from Saint-Sulpice a newly reconsecrated Christian.[19]

In a speech he gave twenty-five years later at a Philadelphia Yearly Meeting of Quakers he explained why he had left the church during the late 1920s and early 1930s. He recalled that the Left then "had a vision, the dream of a classless and war-less world," as the hackneyed phrase goes. This also was a strong factor in making me feel that here, in a sense, was the true church. Here was the fellowship drawn together and drawn forward by the Judeo-Christian prophetic vision of a "new earth in which righteousness dwelleth." The now generally despised Christian liberals had had this vision. As neo-orthodoxy took over, that vision was scorned as naive and utopian. The "Kingdom" was something to be realized "beyond history." And again, the Communists are those who are today able to convince vast multitudes that they do cherish the ancient dream of brotherhood realized on earth and have the determination to make it come true. This is a measure of the fall of what is called the Free World. The liberal Christians were never, in my opinion, wrong in cherishing their vision. Their mistake, and in a sense, their crime, was not to see that it was revolutionary in character and demanded revolutionary living and action of those who claimed to be its votaries.[20]

It was after he left the Trotskyites that Muste really began studying Gandhi, as delineated in the book *War without Violence* (1939) by Krishnalal Shridharani. He wrote and talked about the book, and was influential in getting other American pacifists to read it. For him the main contribution of Gandhi to his political ethics wasn't techniques, which he had already worked out for himself through his own experience with labor strife, but rather in Gandhi's example of successfully using nonviolent action in large-scale political situations. Gandhi's achievement of political ends done in a way with which he could agree was enormously encouraging.[21]

In 1936 he rejoined the FOR, and was elected to its National Council and appointed to a paid position as chair of the Committee on Industrial Relations. In 1937, a Presbyterian search committee invited Muste to serve as director of the

Labor Temple in New York City. Founded in 1910 by Presbyterian minister and Social Gospel activist Charles Stelzle, the Labor Temple functioned not only as a church to serve the Lower East Side immigrant population but also as a meeting place for education, social service, and labor organization as well as an open forum for free and tolerant discussions of diverse political positions. An editorial in the *Presbyterian* questioned the appropriateness of appointing a man whose radical politics had made him "an enemy of the cross of Christ" and who had "helped lead men astray." Muste humbly responded that he hoped to "atone for what harm I may have done during the years I was outside the Church." Indeed, his experience as a Marxist prepared him to counter the attractiveness of "the god that failed" as an alternative to Christianity. "The only true God is not the God of impersonal historical or economic forces which 'automatically' . . . redeem society. . . . The true God is the God of love who can and does redeem man. This God is revealed in Jesus Christ." He argued, in fact, that no economic system whether Communist or capitalist can save.[22] Muste extended the outreach of the Labor Temple over the next three years and invited speakers of varying political views (including Dorothy Day of the Catholic Worker on three occasions) to stimulate group conversation. But with the beginning of World War II, he felt called to devote his whole energy to the cause of pacifism and returned to the FOR, initially as cosecretary with John Nevin Sayre in 1940, and after the latter's resignation, as sole director of the organization. That same year he published his first book, *Nonviolence in an Aggressive World*, in which he mounted an extended argument for pacifism and unilateral disarmament, summarizing positions he would maintain for the rest of his life.

Pacifism, he insisted, is rooted in the biblical soil of the Jewish and Christian traditions. In *Nonviolence in an Aggressive*

World, he delineated a "Jewish-Christian legacy" of prophetic faith or "prophetism" that "taught men the infinite value of the individual soul." Like Heschel, he insisted that the god of Jewish-Christian prophetism is a creator, a worker, rather than an absolute utterly removed from mundane affairs or a mind engaged in dispassionate contemplation of them. The god that Moses encountered as a "bush that burned and was not consumed," burned unceasingly because of the oppression that the Egyptian "bosses" inflicted on Jewish laborers. For Moses, the experience of meeting God required him to identify himself with his oppressed kinsmen, and organize them into Brickmakers' Union Number One and then lead them in a walkout from Egypt. For Muste (unlike Heschel), the supreme incarnation of God and greatest of the prophets of this Jewish-Christian tradition was the carpenter of Nazareth. The folksy quality of Muste's language here, and in other essays and articles, exhibited a rhetorical style that came out of his extensive experience with and sympathy for the working class. Making the point that the churches (and synagogues), the labor movement, and democratic equality are interconnected, he asserted that the connection is an ethical one at base: God burns unceasingly with compassion for the oppressed, and so must we.

In Muste's concept of Christianity, faith is based on the revelation that God is love:

> In the first place, the Christian religion has something to say about the nature of the universe, of God. Jesus put it in the simple and human terms which He constantly used, saying, "God is Father, God is Love." If this is more than a form of words, an incantation which gives us a comfortable feeling inside when we repeat it, it must mean that the most real thing in the universe, the most powerful, the most permanent is love. It must follow that every human organization

and institution will be able to endure and to function in the degree that this divine, creative element of love . . . is embodied in it and promoted by it. . . . It follows also from this conception of God that the deepest reality, the most vital force always works quietly, unobtrusively, steadfastly, works through patience and gentleness and humility. God, life in its deepest sense, does not work through thunder, bluster, aggression, strife, whether that strife be labeled offense or defense.[23]

The chief opponent of Muste's pacifism was the prominent ethicist and Union Theological Seminary professor Reinhold Niebuhr. A former member of the FOR, Niebuhr resigned from the organization when he no longer found pacifism credible. He was a leading figure in the theological movement known as "neo-orthodoxy," which criticized the liberal Social Gospel movement of the earlier twentieth century as naively optimistic about the possibility of social reform, given the inveterate sinfulness of humankind. Ironically, Muste was critical of the Social Gospel as well, but because it was not radical enough in its program of reform. He addressed Niebuhr's pessimistic "realism" in several essays, including an "open letter," and reportedly debated him personally at the Union Theological Seminary, although it seems that no written record of this debate has survived. Muste declared that the foundation of Niebuhr's attack on pacifism rested on three charges: his doctrine of human depravity; his view that Jesus's teaching envisages a wholly transcendent and future Kingdom of God; and his contention that a perfectionist ethic has no immediate relevance to the practical political problems of national and international life.

Muste responded to each charge. Regarding the doctrine of human depravity, he observed that Niebuhr overstated the case: "In dealing on the plane of moral conduct with the very real problem of human sin in its proper sense, the extreme neo-orthodox emphasis on human impotence and corruption is a dangerous distortion."[24] But Muste also granted the validity of some of Niebuhr's criticism:

> So often the preachers of love . . . rebuke people for not loving enough, without realizing that the way they themselves wave the word around is an assertion that they're superior and are entitled to make moral judgments on others. Many of those preachers are actually expressing rejection when they speak of "love." That's why, although I often disagree with Reinhold Niebuhr, I do believe there is an element of truth in the reemphasis on the sinful corruption of human beings that has been made by Niebuhr and the other neo-orthodox theologians. Where Niebuhr's judgment is, I think defective, is that he doesn't take account of all the aspects of St. Paul's spiritual paradox, "Where sin abounds, grace much more abounds." Niebuhr cautions us to be constantly aware of the obverse, "Where grace abounds, sin still exists," so that when you think you're being very loving, you may well be hating in subtle ways. . . . I am more hopeful than Niebuhr that we can achieve a social revolution through changing human beings as well as their institutions by making them aware of both the sin and the grace they contain. But I agree with Niebuhr that simply advocating "love" won't do it.[25]

In answer to Niebuhr's charge that the Gospel ethic of Jesus referred only to personal relationships between individuals, and not national policy or international relations, Muste insisted that the dynamic of love is not relegated to individuals alone. There is no scriptural warrant, he argued, for concluding that national governments are exempt from the moral law or that the only national imperative is survival—a sure recipe for the immoral behavior of the absolutist state. "Religious leaders who hold that the nation may not and should not be called upon to be willing to sacrifice in order that mankind may be saved seem to me to share responsibility for the survival of absolutism and totalitarianism."[26]

To the charge that pacifism counseled a form of unattainable perfectionism, he retorted that this objection might cloak the rationalization of fellow Christians who felt disinclined to obey the difficult demands of the Gospel by refusing to renounce war, for example, even though in their hearts they know it is no longer possible to reconcile modern warfare with the Gospel. Lest he be seen as unfairly judging others, Muste hastened to include himself in the charge of evasion: "Yet who among us is not stricken with shame by the knowledge that he, too, is holding back part of the price of complete commitment that God asks?"[27] Finally, he attacked the charge of unrealistic perfectionism by appealing to the historical precedent of the early Quakers, "who realized only too clearly that the Kingdom of God had not come but who had an inward sense that it *would never come* until somebody believed in its principles enough to try them in actual operation."[28] Nor would a perfect social order ever be established. Like Rauschenbusch, Muste believed that "the kingdom is always but coming," an ever-beckoning beacon of light amid the darkness of indifference, inaction, and despair.

Seven years later, he delineated the religious roots of pacifism in a second book, *Not by Might: Christianity, the Way to Human Decency and of Holy Disobedience.* The title came from the biblical prophet Zechariah (4:16): "Not by might, nor by power, but by my spirit." Muste dedicated the book with personal urgency to his and everyone's grandchildren: "With the prayer that the people may renounce the sin and folly of war so that we may not sacrifice our grandchildren as we have our children to this Moloch of our supreme and suicidal devotion." In this text, he defined the redemptive power of nonviolent suffering as an expression of the divine love at the center of history: "It is well known that you can crucify the man of conscience, of complete moral integrity, but that when you do so you have not destroyed or diminished the power that was in him and flowed through him. Rather, you have performed an act even more stupendous than that of splitting the atom: you have unleashed power that will 'destroy this temple' but will also 'in three days build it again'; that will end an age and a civilization and build another."[29] Muste stressed that pacifism was rooted not only in belief but also in concomitant behavior. And emulating Gandhi, he did not shrink from describing the painful cost of pacifist behavior:

> If the ultimate expression of violence is killing the opponent, the "aggressor," the ultimate expression of nonviolence or soul force is quite as obviously the willingness and ability to die at the hands and on behalf of the evildoer. The pacifist must be ready to pay that price. . . . The suffering need not be sought. Indeed it must not be. Martyrdom for the sake of martyrdom is suicide by exhibitionism, not redemptive crucifixion. But we may not seek to evade suffering. It must be voluntarily accepted. The model for accepting such sacrifice is passion and death. . . . Then God has entered into history and its course has been forever changed. Here is released the power which in the political and social realm is the counterpart of the fission of the atom and the release of atomic energy in its realm. If the Christian religion means anything, it means this. If the experience of mankind has taught anything, it teaches this.[30]

For Muste, then, at the center of pacifism lies the iconic symbol of the cross of Christ, whereas the iconic symbol of violence is the atomic bomb.

During World War II, Muste protested not only war making but also conscription, and counseled draft resisters and assisted those imprisoned for refusal to register. Moreover, he repeatedly appealed to the White House to act on the plight of European Jews, calling for expansion of US immigrant quotas and stepped-up efforts to bring threatened refugees to this country. He warned President Franklin Delano Roosevelt and other federal officials, in September 1943, that "unless something is done soon virtually none of the Jews native to Poland and Germany and who are still there or in other Axis-held territory will survive the winter." No reply was recorded. He protested the obliteration bombing of cities that resulted in massive civilian casualties. Of the atomic bombing of Hiroshima and Nagasaki, he caustically observed: "It was the United States, 'Christian America,' which perpetrated the atrocities. It was we and not the Nazi swine as they were called, the Fascist devils, the Japanese militarists or the Russian communists."[31] In the wake of Dresden, Hiroshima, and Nagasaki, Muste pleaded with the church to exercise its prophetic vocation by clearly condemning all warfare:

> Men are waiting to have the Church tell them in Christ's name whether making atomic war is right or wrong. . . . [A] clear and unequivocal answer, a command coming out of pulpits and church schools and confessionals saying, "War is no longer, if it ever was, distinguishable from murder. If you claim to be a Christian, you can no more take part in it than in chattel slavery" . . . this men would recognize as the sound of a voice not their own, "in the existence of which we cannot disbelieve." For it would be God speaking as of old through the prophets and through His Christ.[32]

The development of the atom and hydrogen bombs along with the ensuing arms race resulting in the proliferation of nuclear weapons prompted Muste to warn against the increasing possibility of overwhelming human destruction. He had no sympathy for the realpolitik of deterrence: "Threatening to use nuclear weapons if we mean in some circumstances to use them . . . is in the form of preparation to commit an obscene atrocity. If, on the other hand, we really mean never to use them, then keeping up the threat is deceitful. It contributes to confusion and distrust in a tense and troubled world."[33]

Furthermore, the imbalance between military spending and funding for the poor in the United States and internationally was a moral disgrace. On materialism, one of the three evil triplets, alongside racism and militarism, he remarked, "We can overcome materialism only by renouncing it and practicing brotherhood."[34] Muste understood that unilateral disarmament seemed like a quixotic ideal to the vast majority of the public, but persisted in hoping that it was possible. Ultimately, his strategic goal was to develop

> concerted, persistent, powerful efforts by pacifists in all lands to increase the number of conscientious objectors and to bring about disarmament by their own respective nations . . . a movement for universal disarmament brought about by the conquest of fear and by the spirit of love for mankind. In such a movement there is hope as there is not in any movement for general disarmament depending on mutual fear of each nation for the others and on fear of the atomic bomb. Such preaching as we are advocating is, of course, religious preaching in content, in inspiration, in basis. . . . I do not refer to a verbal profession of religion; not to this or that dogmatic formulation; nor to adherence to this or that ecclesiastical institution. I do mean a pacifism rooted in a certain conception of the nature of life, the universe, God; to a pacifism which is an inner experience, an inner attitude toward life, hence a way of life, and not merely a tool or device which the individual uses in certain circumstances on his environment. One

must not only favor pacifism or nonviolence as a policy in such and such circumstances, one must be a pacifist.[35]

Lest such a daunting task seem impossible, Muste prescribed trust in God: "At this crucial moment in human history, in the presence of such responsibility, we 'upon whom the end of the age has come' stand humbled yet not cast down. God, who places the responsibility upon His children, gives also in overflowing measure the power to accomplish the work—the God 'in whose will,' in [Saint] Augustine's great words, 'is our peace' and the peace of the stricken, war-ravished world."[36]

In the midst of his antinuclear activities, Anna, who had for years suffered from a heart condition, died in September 1954. Muste would continue the struggle without his wife of forty-five years. His main "weapons" were the pen, platform, and movement. In March 1956, the first issue of *Liberation* magazine appeared. It quickly became the most comprehensive and widely read source of information about movements to abolish colonialism, racism, and all forms of domination. Over time, the journal would report on the landmark episodes in social action in the 1950s and 1960s—civil rights campaigns, atomic testing protests, antinuclear missile demonstrations, and the anti–Vietnam War movement. *Liberation* became Muste's "chief public forum, the one place where his writings would appear regularly throughout the last decade of his life."[37]

His institutional base remained the FOR. Regarding his leadership style, one who knew it well observed,

> A. J. was national secretary of the Fellowship, which meant national director. Although he was clearly the dominant spokesperson for the organization, everyone in the office was treated more like a member of a large family than as a worker with assigned tasks. Pacifists during the war were drawn together

by their convictions, and A. J. was simply another one of us, though even then his writings and speeches sometimes reached beyond the ranks of the pacifist community. He seemed to live, breathe and constantly practice nonviolence, on occasion even to the neglect of more mundane matters.[38]

Along with Dorothy Day of the *Catholic Worker*, whom he had met in 1937, Muste led repeated demonstrations against mandatory participation in annual civil defense drills in New York City, refusing to obey the air raid signal to move into the designated bomb shelters. Hauled before the court, he and other demonstrators were fined and occasionally jailed for these acts of civil disobedience.

Day later recalled these times fondly when reading Nat Hentoff's book *Peace Agitator: The Story of the Life of A. J. Muste* led her to reminisce in the pages of the *Catholic Worker* in March 1964:

> The last time I saw A. J. Muste was on the anniversary of Hiroshima last August when he started the sit-down in front of the Atomic Energy Commission. Along the curb was a long line of peace lovers, pacifists who stood by, and faced by a barricade of police, A. J. Muste sat, not too easily, cross legged on the ground, a small pillow protecting his thin shanks. He is a long lean man. Even so it must have been painful penance. I contemplated him as I stood for a while with the line, and thought of [Winston] Churchill and of Muste, almost of an age, in the sight of God who stands higher? There is no doubt in my mind as to which is the more significant figure.[39]

Muste countered objections that demonstrations were unrealistic:

> Actually [they are] an important element in the peace education of great numbers of people. [They also give] a positive

and active connotation to the term "pacifist." The cumulative effect of all these projects and vigils is to bring into work for peace thousands of people who would never before have thought of engaging in any sort of demonstration. A movement becomes very different in character and in its effect on the non-committed when it can get people out onto the street confronting authority. Also, demonstrations bring us much more publicity than any other technique. I do not say that nonviolent action is the only form of useful action for peace, but it's an extremely important part of the educative process that is our essential aim.[40]

His total commitment to the example of civil disobedience led him to Mead Air Force Base, outside Omaha, Nebraska, in 1959. At the age of seventy-four, Muste hoisted his frail frame over a four-and-a-half-foot fence. After a written warning he was arrested, spent eight days in jail, and received a suspended sentence of six months, a $500 fine, plus one year of probation. Soon afterward, he supported a protest against the Polaris nuclear submarine in New London, Connecticut, but didn't physically participate due to his probation and other commitments. On another front, he actively took part in organizing and gaining support for a San Francisco to Moscow peace walk in 1960–61, which involved him traveling to Russia to engage in negotiations for the marchers to enter. After they did march in Red Square, Muste exclaimed that the march had been "an Experiment in Truth and Nonviolence in the Gandhian tradition."[41]

Although Muste was not a civil rights leader, he served an extremely important role as an adviser for and enabler of several crucial civil rights organizations, and a keen analyst of the relationship between nonviolence and the struggle for racial equality. Martin Luther King Jr. acknowledged his contribution to the movement in a telegram he sent to Muste in February 1965 on the occasion of his eightieth birthday: "You have climbed the mountain and have seen the great and abiding truth to which you have dedicated your life. Throughout the world you are honored as our most effective exponent of pacifism. You have been a great friend and inspiration to me and the whole nonviolent movement. Without you the American Negro might never have caught the meaning of true love for humanity."[42] According to civil rights veterans Glenn Smiley, James Lawson, and James Farmer, King had just cause to make these remarks. Farmer stressed that while Muste had not been in the thick of the civil rights struggle, he had played a key role in the early stages of the Congress of Racial Equality (CORE), and through others, had helped strengthen the pacifism of King. Bayard Rustin and Smiley had been especially significant in this regard during the Montgomery bus boycott. Lawson cited the importance of Muste's influence on himself, Farmer, Rustin, Randolph, and finally the prominent black clergyman and philosopher Howard Thurman, who joined the FOR in 1917. Thurman credited Muste with having a role in his leaving Howard University in 1943 to copastor the Church of the Fellowship of All Peoples. It was Muste who forwarded to Thurman, by then a member of the FOR board, a letter asking for the names of potential candidates to minister to an interracial church in San Francisco.[43]

Moreover, Muste used his position at the FOR to encourage members of his staff to engage in civil rights organizing. Farmer, who became the national director of CORE, was allowed to spend time on developing CORE by the FOR with Muste's support. George Houser and Rustin also spent time building up the organization of CORE, with Houser serving for most of the 1940s as its executive director. Both organized

the first "freedom ride" in 1947 as "the journey of reconciliation," cosponsored by the FOR and CORE. Lawson helped to
organize the 1960 Nashville sit-ins, which got him expelled
from the Vanderbilt Divinity School. He credited Muste with
helping to awaken his interest in nonviolence. When he first
heard Muste lecture at Vanderbilt, he had been impressed
by how gently he handled a violent heckler, besides making
good sense.[44]

Rustin, who became a close advisee of Muste, remembered that

> he was so productive a leader because he was so realistic.
> What some have called his saintliness is combined with unu-
> sual political shrewdness. He also knows and admits enough
> of the existence of evil not to share the easy optimism of
> the average pacifist. . . . I learned more about nonviolence
> from him than in all my subsequent reading. . . . The social
> institutions—as well as man himself—had to be changed. . . .
> You have to act, and act with your body, in nonviolent
> demonstrations to create social dislocation. I carried over his
> lessons to my later work with Martin Luther King. . . . Muste
> himself has always been willing to go to jail for his principles,
> and those principles are remarkably consistent.[45]

Muste's insistence on nonviolence led him to publish in
the May 1964 issue of *Liberation* an essay titled "Rifle Squads
or the Beloved Community," in which he urged volunteers in
training for the Mississippi Freedom Summer project to organize and demonstrate without relying on federal troops for
protection. Printed copies of that essay were stacked on the
literature table at the Ohio college campus where summer
volunteers gathered in June for orientation before setting out
for the state of Mississippi to indeed face physical violence
and even death, without protection of federal law officers and

with local police actually colluding in the murder of three young civil rights workers, James Chaney, Andrew Goodman, and Michael Schwerner.[46]

In fall 1964, Muste joined a select group of peace activists in a retreat called the Spiritual Roots of Protest at the Trappist Monastery of Our Lady of Gethsemani, in Kentucky, hosted by Thomas Merton. Monasticism with its ascetic otherworldliness was antithetical to Muste's Reformed and Quaker sensibilities as well as his commitment to reforming this world rather than retreating from it for the sake of the next. "My own vocation," he noted, "has certainly not been to asceticism as it is usually understood. This is because I have a deep-seated conviction that the aim and the essence of life is love. And love is in its inmost nature an affirmation, not a negation; an embracing and being embraced, not rejections and withdrawal."[47] He respected Day and the "this worldly" activism of the Catholic Worker movement she led, precisely because of its direct service to the urban poor. And he had worked with some of the younger Catholic pacifists, such as Jim Forest, who created the Catholic Peace Fellowship within the FOR. But his visit to Gethsemani took him into an unfamiliar territory of silent solitude and otherworldly asceticism. "To my sorrow," remembered Tom Cornell of the Catholic Peace Fellowship, Muste "never once went to hear the choir monks chant the Divine Office." But he did "walk in the woods to Merton's secluded hermitage over wet autumn leaves, dangerously slippery," with younger retreatants "hovering behind him as inconspicuously as possible to scoop him up if he fell, like angels commissioned lest he dash his foot against a stone." For the better part of two days the assembled activists, including the Catholic priests Philip and Daniel Berrigan, the Mennonite ethicist John Howard Yoder, Wilbur Ferry of the Center for the Study of

Democratic Institutions, Forest and Cornell of the Catholic Worker and the Catholic Peace Fellowship, former FOR director John Oliver Nelson, and FOR's director of education John C. Heidbrink, discussed the spiritual roots and personal implications of their protest against war and other forms of violence. Muste was impressed with Merton's "really very brilliant mind," and called his visit "a very illuminating and encouraging experience." "One feels no restraint in his presence," he commented. Yet he wondered how Merton managed to endure life in a Trappist monastery. Unfortunately, it seems that Muste had not read Merton's own renunciation of a "spurious monastic separatism" nor his perceptive antiwar, anticonsumerism, and antiracism essays. If he had, he might have understood how much the monk's contemplative vision led to his prophetic social vision. Muste, recently recuperated from cataract surgery, was, according to Cornell, "happy as a boy looking at everything to be seen as we drove from the airport at Lexington through the knobby Kentucky hills to the Abbey."[48]

Long after the age when most of his contemporaries retired, Muste continued an exhausting pace of protest activity. He traveled the country and world; spent time in jail for demonstrations against nuclear weapons; wrote in defense of the growing civil rights movement in the US South and offered sage advice to its leaders; warned against the dangers of Cold War brinkmanship; and articulated the need for liberation struggles in India, Africa, and Latin America to proceed nonviolently. Muste sought funds for nonviolent causes, and remained available to assist his fellow activists in trouble politically or personally. He never ceased being a pastor. "One of Muste's remarkable qualities the last year of his life," observed David Dellinger, "was his ability to learn from even the humblest, least experienced and most confused with whom he worked." He knew, Dellinger explained, how "to bring his own wisdom to [an] encounter, without being enslaved by it or intimidating others with it. There was seldom a strategy session of the organizations he headed, in which most of the others did not speak before he did," a patience learned, perhaps, from his experience of silent worship in Quaker meetings that customarily permitted each person moved by the spirit to speak until the clerk of the meeting concluded by summarizing "the sense of the meeting."[49] For Rustin, Muste's capacity for joyous involvement in whatever the present moment offered was exemplified in an incident they shared in India, when Rustin roused the elderly Muste from his sleep to meet a band of gypsies who had come into the village where they were staying, with the result that Muste danced until dawn with his new friends. Muste's availability did have a downside. Besides physical exhaustion, the constant demands of different organizations prevented him from providing the stability required to build a constituency for a unified movement—a failure he always regretted.[50] Habitually serving many causes, he had no time to lead one.

Always enmeshed in dealing with various bureaucracies, he still kept sight of the personal touch, as a birthday letter attested:

> The wife of a man who had been a conscientious objector during the Second World War added a handwritten note to her husband's birthday letter to Muste. "Let the others sing your praises for your courage, intelligence, energy and great spiritual fortitude. I sing your praises because you were and are the kind of man who—on a Christmas Day of a busy war year—could take the time to write a word of good cheer and love to a lonely wife whose husband was in prison. It is the two sides of you put together that brings joy to the heart."[51]

The last years of Muste's life were preoccupied by the war in Vietnam. "I can't get it out of my head or my guts that Americans are away over there not only shooting at people but dropping bombs on them, roasting them with napalm and all the rest." Not content with demonstrating against the war at home, he traveled, at the age of eighty-one, on a peace mission to Saigon in 1966. There he and his colleagues were heckled at a public meeting by hired agents of the South Vietnamese government—a signal of its opposition to their presence. Against the advice of his doctors, Muste traveled with a small delegation to Hanoi at the age of eighty-two in January 1967. His group received a warm welcome from Ho Chi Minh, and toured the city and bombed-out countryside. Ho Chi Minh asked him to carry a personal invitation to President Lyndon Baines Johnson to meet for personal negotiations to end the war.[52] Exhausted by the trip, Muste did not rest but instead continued his active schedule as usual. On a Saturday morning, February 11, he complained of extreme pain in his back. When medication failed to help, he was taken by ambulance to St. Luke's hospital, where he died later that afternoon of an aneurysm. He was cremated two days later and interred besides his wife, Anna, in Ferncliff Cemetery in Ardsley, New York.

At Muste's memorial service at the Community Church, two of his favorite poems, both by Stephen Spender, were read, including "The Truly Great":

> I think continually of those who were truly great.
> Who, from the womb, remembered the soul's history
> Through corridors of light where the hours are suns
> Endless and singing. Whose lovely ambition
> Was that their lips, still touched with fire,
> Should tell of the Spirit clothed from head to foot in song.

And who hoarded from the Spring branches
The desires falling across their bodies like blossoms.
What is precious is never to forget
The essential delight of the blood drawn from ageless springs
Breaking through rocks in worlds before our earth.
Never to deny its pleasure in the morning simple light
Nor its grave evening demand for love.
Never to allow gradually the traffic to smother
With noise and fog the flowering of the spirit.
Near the snow, near the sun, in the highest fields
See how these names are fêted by the waving grass
And by the streamers of white cloud
And whispers of wind in the listening sky.
The names of those who in their lives fought for life
Who wore at their hearts the fire's centre.
Born of the sun they traveled a short while towards the sun,
And left the vivid air signed with their honor.

Condolence messages poured in from near and far to the offices of the FOR and *Liberation*, demonstrating Muste's international influence. Ho Chi Minh, Robert Kennedy, Erich Fromm, and heads of various peace organizations from South Africa, Japan, Tanzania, Israel, Paris, Saint Petersburg, and British Columbia paid their respects to Muste. In a memorial column in the *Catholic Worker*, Day lamented the passing of her fellow against arms and celebrated his life's work:

The Rev. A. J. Muste, known to all of us in the peace movement as A. J., is dead. The name Abraham means Father of a multitude, and he was that. If the peace movement in the United States had one outstanding figure it was A. J., and God gave him length of days to work. He was eighty-two years old when he died and many of us had seen him that last week of his life. Tuesday, the day of the blizzard, A. J. and sixty-one others were due to appear in court at Centre Street, to answer to a number of charges, beginning with "breach of the peace" and "conspiring to commit breach of the peace." In addition, there was a warrant out for A. J.'s arrest for failing to show up for one of the previous hearings on this charge. He had been in Hanoi at the time talking to Ho Chi Minh. . . . The offense had been committed on December 15th and it was now February 7th and he had been around the world in that time, traveling to the ends of the earth, one might say, in search of peace. . . . Peter Maurin and I first met him when he took over the directorship of the old Presbyterian Labor Temple where he served from 1937 to 1940. As I remember it, the Labor Temple on the corner of Fourteenth Street and Second Avenue, functioned then as Community Church does now, and Peter Maurin felt that here was a beginning of what he called a new synthesis, an attempt to apply the teachings of the Gospel to the world today, the world around us. Above all, A. J. felt that war could not be reconciled with the spirit of Christ. "War does not bring peace, it merely breeds more wars," he said. The thing that marked him especially was his relationship to the young. He listened to them and they listened to him, well "over thirty" though he was. He never judged the young, nor criticized them. He criticized the social order and by his writing as well as by his actions, tried to bring about a change in that social order. He walked on picket lines, he trespassed on missile bases, he was to be found in courtrooms and in jails as well as in the lecture hall and behind the editorial desk. He truly worked to make that kind of a world where it is easier to be good.[53]

Figure 3.1 Dorothy Day. Photographer: Diana Jo Davies. Courtesy of the Department of Special Collections and University Archives, Marquette University Libraries.

Figure 3.2 Peter Maurin. Courtesy of the Department of Special Collections and University Archives, Marquette University Libraries.

CHAPTER 3

DOROTHY DAY AND THE
CATHOLIC WORKER MOVEMENT
DOING THE WORKS OF MERCY

> Love in action is a harsh and dreadful thing compared
> to love in dreams.
>
> — Fyodor Dostoyevsky,
> *The Brothers Karamazov*

DURING HOLY WEEK IN 1961, my freshman year of college at Loyola University in Los Angeles, I went on a retreat with a small group of classmates to Valyermo, a small Benedictine monastery near Palm Desert, California. There was another retreatant staying at the monastery, an older woman, named Dorothy Day. I had started reading her newspaper, the *Catholic Worker*, when I was fifteen, and knew of her outspoken commitment to serving the poor and protesting war. In fact, reading the *Catholic Worker* had prompted me to engage a couple of guys in my dorm in a heated discussion about the immorality of bombing Hiroshima and Nagasaki. The retreat master asked her to address our group, and she agreed. One evening, in a calm yet firm voice, she proceeded to condemn the nuclear arms race and insist that the United States should unilaterally disarm. Disturbed by her talk—it was, after all, the height of the Cold War and seemed unthinkable to disarm in the face of Soviet missiles—we were too shy to challenge her moral authority, but after her talk we asked the retreat master for his opinion. After a short pause, he responded, "Well, I am sure that one day Dorothy Day will be declared a saint, but, were I President [John F.] Kennedy, I wouldn't take her advice." Later, as I learned more about her and the activities of the movement she cofounded with Peter Maurin, I understood that her refrain "Don't call me a saint" was not just a protest of humility but instead a rejection of being marginalized as an impractical idealist. "Don't call me a saint. I don't want to be dismissed so easily." The tension I felt at seventeen between the assumptions of my comfortable life and the unsettling implications of her demand for radical personal, political, and social change has remained a nagging challenge ever since.

Born in Bath Beach, Brooklyn, a few blocks from the bridge, on November 8, 1897, Dorothy May Day was the third of five children; she had three brothers and a sister. Her father, John Day, was a newspaper sports columnist, who covered horse racing. Distant with his children, and a self-proclaimed atheist who always carried a Bible, he would refer to his grown daughter as "the nut of the family." Her mother, Grace Satterlee Day, was a homemaker and close to her daughter, but also restrained in expressing emotion. Both of Dorothy's older brothers became journalists. With her younger sister, Della, she enjoyed a lifelong closeness, as she did with her little brother, John Jr. The family didn't attend church or practice religion at home.

In 1904, they moved to Oakland, California, so her father could take a job as a sportswriter for a San Francisco paper. The San Francisco earthquake devastated the city in 1906, and destroyed her father's newspaper plant and livelihood. The earthquake left a lasting impression on the nine-year-old Dorothy, especially the acts of kindness she witnessed as her mother and neighbors offered food, clothes, and shelter to the victims of the catastrophe. She never forgot the feeling of community and shared sacrifice with those in need. Her father decided to search for work in Chicago. Initially he was unable to find anything, and they were forced to live in a row house in a poor area of the city, where Dorothy came in contact with immigrants and the laboring poor. One day, a chance encounter with the mother of one of her playmates sparked an unexpected interest in religion:

> It was around ten o'clock in the morning that I went up to Kathryn's house to call for her to come out and play. There was no one on the porch or in the kitchen. The breakfast dishes had all been washed. . . . Thinking the children must be in the front room, I burst in [and] ran through the bedrooms. In the front bedroom Mrs. Barrett was on her knees, saying her prayers. She turned to tell me that Kathryn and the children had all gone to the store and went on with her praying. I felt a burst of love toward Mrs. Barrett that I have never forgotten, a feeling of gratitude and happiness that warmed my heart. She had God, and there was beauty and joy in her life. All through my life what she was doing remained with me. And though I became oppressed with the problem of poverty and injustice, though I groaned at the hideous sordidness of man's lot, though there were years when I clung to the philosophy of economic determinism as an explanation of man's fate, still there were moments when in the midst of misery and class strife, life was shot through with glory. Mrs. Barrett in her sordid little tenement flat finished her breakfast dishes at ten o'clock in the morning and got down on her knees and prayed to God.[1]

Her formal participation in religion began when the pastor of the local Episcopal Church persuaded her parents to send four of their children to Sunday services. Dorothy came to love the Psalms and prayers. Years later in her autobiography, *The Long Loneliness*, she recalled, "I had never heard anything as beautiful as the Benedicite and the Te Deum. . . . The song thrilled in my heart, and though I was only ten years old, through these Psalms and canticles I called on all creation to join with me in blessing the Lord."[2]

By the age of fifteen, Day was an avid reader, absorbed in the works of Jack London, Upton Sinclair, and Peter Kropotkin. She stopped going to church, being "sick and tired of religion." Reading the books of London and Sinclair had led her to distrust all churches, but she continued to believe in God and read the New Testament. She began taking long walks in the poorer sections on Chicago's West Side, fascinated by the glimpses of immigrant life, smells of food cooking in kitchens, and color of vegetable patches carefully tended in small yards. (All her life, Day would appreciate the small beauties of poor urban neighborhoods.) When her father finally landed a job as sports editor of the *Inter Ocean*, they could afford to move to a better neighborhood on the North Side. In June 1914, Day graduated from high school, and won a $300 scholarship prize for achievement in Latin and Greek. That fall she enrolled at the University of Illinois. An indifferent student, with a rebellious attitude, she exercised the freedom to do what she wanted—"to deny convention when it suited her." Lonely and homesick, she decided that one of her professors was right when he remarked that religion is "for the weak." To prove her independence of convention, she began to curse, smoke, and cut classes, spending her time reading whatever she wanted: labor history, the novels of Ivan Turgenev, Maxim Gorky, Anton Chekhov, Leo Tolstoy, and Dostoyevsky—so establishing a lasting devotion to Russian literature and especially Dostoyevsky. She worked menial jobs to support herself and finally found friendship as a member of the Scribblers, a literary composition group on campus.

When her family moved to New York City so her father could take a job for the *Morning Telegraph* after the *Inter Ocean* folded, she joined them, dropping out of college after two years. Against her father's wishes, she found work as a journalist for a succession of radical periodicals including the *Call*, the *Masses* (until it was suppressed by the government), and later the *Liberator*. At the age of eighteen, she moved out of her parents' home to live on the Lower East Side in a series of cheap, run-down apartments. In 1917, she accompanied a group of women demonstrating for women's suffrage in Washington, DC, and got arrested and jailed for the first time. The prisoners staged a hunger strike before their release on pardon by President Woodrow Wilson. Day was never a card-carrying member of any Socialist movement, but "maintained her college . . . enthusiasm for whomever she regarded as a victim of merciless capital."[3] During the next three years, she participated actively in the bohemian life of the East Village. She hung out, frequently in bars, with journalists, intellectuals, and perhaps most notably the Provincetown players and Eugene O'Neill, with whom she developed a close relationship. His black moods and uncanny ability to recite from memory, while drunk, the entire poem "The Hound of Heaven" by Francis Thompson left a lasting impression on her.

World War I, the Spanish flu pandemic of 1918, and guilt that she only wrote about social injustice but did nothing to change it, moved her to enroll in a rigorous training program for nurses in 1920. In the hospital she met and became obsessed with Lionel Moise, a womanizing journalist, who promised no commitment that would restrict his freedom.

She got pregnant and had an abortion in desperate hope that he would stay with her—to no avail. Moise didn't even bother to pick her up after the abortion and left her a letter, saying she should forget him and find some rich guy to marry. Abandoned and deeply depressed, she made two attempts at suicide. Several months later she married Barkeley Tobey, a much-older wealthy businessman. They traveled to Europe, where she left him and holed up for a year in Capri writing a thinly veiled autobiographical novel, *The Eleventh Virgin*. The book finished, she returned to the States and succeeded in getting her novel published (to lukewarm reviews) in 1924. A Hollywood film studio bought the rights, and with the money she purchased a small cottage on the west end of Staten Island, where she lived from 1925 until 1929. Through mutual friends, she met and fell in love with Forster (Foster) Batterham. They decided to live together and contracted a common law marriage. Batterham was a biologist, atheist, and anarchist, who rejected religion and the restrictions of social conventions. Again Day got pregnant and was blissful: "For a long time I had thought I could not bear a child, and the longing in my heart for a baby had been growing. . . . I felt myself unfruitful, barren." She felt that some disease of her soul had been cured, that God had forgiven her, and a pall that had hung over her had been removed. "I had not known real freedom nor even a knowledge of what freedom meant." She began to pray the rosary (given her by a Catholic friend) on her walk in the morning to get the mail. "Maybe I did not say it correctly, but I kept on saying it because it made me happy. . . . No matter how dull the day, nor long the walk . . . the words I had been saying insinuated themselves into my heart before I had finished, so that . . . I was filled with exultation." She began visiting a nearby Catholic chapel. After reading Thomas à Kempis's *Imitation of Christ*, she resolved to have her child baptized. And Day prayed for the gift of faith for herself.[4]

Forster's reaction to her pregnancy was initially negative. He didn't want the responsibility of a child and was especially resentful of Day's growing interest in religion. Day clearly identified the proximate cause of her conversion with the birth of her daughter, Tamar Teresa:

> "When one has a child, life is different. Certainly I did not want my child to flounder as I had often floundered, 'without a rule of life, an instruction.' She had no doubts that it would be the Catholic Church in which she wanted her daughter to be raised, in large part because it "held the allegiance of the masses of people in all the cities where I had lived." It was the immigrant church of the laboring class that appealed deeply to Day, the socially concerned activist, devoted to the poor, the laborer, and the immigrant since her youth.[5]

Her conversion was also influenced by her sacramental view of nature. She wrote of her experience on Staten Island in 1925: "I was born again by the word of the Spirit, contemplating the beauty of the sea and the shore, wind and waves, the tides. The mighty and the minute, the storms and peace, wave and the wavelets of receding tides, sea gulls, and seaweed, and shells, all gave testimony of a Creator, a Father almighty made known to us through His Son."[6] Tragically, the very love of nature, which formed such a strong bond with Forster, led to the breaking of that connection. Of their relationship, she later observed:

> It was human love that helped me to understand divine love. Human love, at its best, unselfish, glowing, illuminating our days, gives us a glimpse of the love of God for man. When one is in love, one cannot conceive of not being in love. Life

seems dull and drab to contemplate without this vital emotion. Love is the best thing we can know in this life, but it
must be sustained by an effort of the will. You are conscious
always of the presence in this world with you of another
human being who is bound to you in some strange way, by
some spell, so that you are obsessed by the thought of him.
But what about God? I wonder am I continually conscious,
in the background of my thought, of His presence in my life?
Am I practicing the presence of God, as the phrase is? Because of God is each task ennobled, each contact vivified,
each moment more intense? Is the love of Christ, in other
words, driving me on?[7]

It was not because I was tired of sex, satiated, disillusioned, that I turned to God. Radical friends used to insinu-
ate this. It was because through a whole love, both physical
and spiritual, I came to know God.[8]

Her separation from Forster, painful and drawn out,
became final due to her decision to be baptized. It was a
wrenching choice, and she continued to keenly feel his absence, trying to persuade him to marry her for several years
after the separation. She felt that she faced a life-changing
choice between God and man; she chose God. On December
28, 1927, she was baptized into the Roman Catholic Church
at the age of thirty. She experienced no consolation, no joy,
in the reception of the sacrament. It was unemotional—a determined act of will. Moreover, she was acutely aware that
her baptism would break her relationships with her radical
friends, whose views she shared of the institutional church as
supporter of property, the wealthy, the state, capitalism, and
all the forces of reaction. Had she "sold out"?

I loved the Church for Christ made visible. Not for itself,
because it was so often a scandal to me. Romano Guardini

said the Church is the Cross on which Christ was crucified; one could not separate Christ from His Cross, and one must live in a state of permanent dissatisfaction with the Church. The scandal of businesslike priests, of collective wealth, the lack of a sense of responsibility for the poor, the worker, the Negro, the Mexican, the Filipino, and even the oppression of these, and the consenting to the oppression of them by our industrialist-capitalist order—these made me feel often that priests were more like Cain than Abel.[9]

She continued to write for the Anti-Imperialist League and then found a job with the Fellowship of Reconciliation (FOR). She remained a lifelong member of the FOR. In 1929, Pathé Studio hired Day to come to Los Angeles as a script dialogue writer at a high salary. But there was not much for her to do, and after three months, the studio did not renew her contract. She and Tamar moved to Mexico, where she wrote articles for *Commonweal* and *America*, two leading Catholic journals, including beautiful descriptions of the folk Catholicism of Mexico. After returning to New York, she took an assignment covering the December 1932 hunger march on Washington, DC—a march organized by the Communist-led Unemployed Councils to protest unemployment, demand relief, and condemn evictions.

The absence of Catholic participation in the hunger strike troubled her conscience: Where were the bishops, priests, and laypeople of the church? After the march, she went to the Basilica of the Immaculate Conception (fittingly, it was December 8, the Feast of the Immaculate Conception): "There I offered up a special prayer, a prayer which came with tears and with anguish, that some way would open up for me to use what talents I possessed for my fellow workers, for the poor. And when I returned to New York, I found Peter Maurin—Peter the French peasant, whose spirit and ideas [would] dominate the rest of my life."[10] Her experience in journalism, socialist concern for the poor, love of literature, omnivorous reading, familiarity with protest techniques, and critical perspectives on society's injustice had fitted her—thanks to the unlikely catalyst of Maurin—to lead a movement.

Aristide Peter Maurin was born into a peasant family in Oultet, a tiny mountain village in the Languedoc region of southern France, on May 9, 1877. He was the oldest in a family of twenty-two children, whose history traced back to centuries of farming the land. Educated by the Congregation of Christian Brothers, he joined that order at the age of sixteen. In 1902, when the French government closed many religious schools, Maurin left the Christian Brothers and became active in Le Sillon, a Catholic lay movement that advocated Christian democracy, and supported cooperatives and unions. In 1908, disenchanted with the movement's increasingly political character, Maurin resigned from Le Sillon, and in 1909 he emigrated to Canada, probably to escape the draft. For two years he homesteaded in Saskatchewan, until his partner was killed in an accident. Afterward he took whatever work he could find, first in Canada, and then in the United States—digging ditches, quarrying stone, harvesting wheat, cutting lumber, and laying track. He worked in brickyards, steel mills, and coal mines. In 1932, he found a job as a handyman at a Catholic boys' camp in upstate New York, receiving meals, use of the chaplain's library, and living space in the barn. Through his years of reflection and hard labor, Maurin came to embrace poverty as a gift from God. His unencumbered life offered time for study and prayer, out of which a vision had taken shape—a vision of a social order instilled with the basic values of the Gospel "in which it would be easier for men to be good." As often as his work allowed, he traveled to New York City, staying in cheap Bowery hotels. He spent his days either at the public library or sitting in city parks expounding his ideas to anyone who showed interest. To him, "the way to reach the man on the street is meet the man on the street." He met George Shuster, editor of *Commonweal* magazine, who gave him Day's address, suggesting they had similar ideas. At the time they met, Maurin was fifty-seven and Day was thirty-five.

To many, Maurin seemed just one more eccentric street-corner orator, or a gregarious bum with a thick French accent. Day quickly came to regard him as the answer to her prayers, as someone who could help her discover what she was supposed to do. Maurin, in turn, saw Day as a new Saint Catherine of Siena, and believed that like her medieval predecessor, she would "move mountains, and have influence on governments, temporal and spiritual." But first she needed a truly Catholic education. Maurin wanted her to look at history in a new way—centered not on the rise and fall of nations but rather on the lives of the saints. She had to understand that sanctity was what really mattered, and that any program of social change must emphasize sanctity and community. Maurin proposed that Day start a newspaper to publicize Catholic social teaching and promote steps to bring about the peaceful transformation of society. Day responded positively, though unsure how she would ever find the money for such a venture. "In the history of the saints," Maurin assured her, "capital is raised by prayer. God sends you what you need when you need it. You will be able to pay the printer. Just read the lives of the saints."[11]

The name Maurin proposed for the paper was the *Catholic Radical*. A radical (from the Latin word *radix*, meaning root) is someone who doesn't settle for cosmetic solutions, he said, but goes to the root of personal and social problems. Day felt that the name should refer to the class of readers she hoped the paper would attract and so named it the *Catholic Worker*. "Man proposes and woman disposes," Maurin meekly responded. When the first issue of the paper was ready for distribution on May 1, 1933, however, Maurin asked that his name be excluded from the list of editors. He found the paper short on ideas, principles, and strategy for building a new social order. Apart from his own blank verse called "Easy Essays," and a few quotations from the Bible and papal encyclicals, the rest of the paper struck him as just one more journal of radical protest. The *Catholic Worker* began with twenty-five hundred copies. Within three years, its circulation rose to a hundred thousand, and today it is ninety thousand.

When, in a moment of dejection, Day asked Maurin, why people were so resistant to change, he responded soberly, "People are just beginning to realize how deep-seated the evil is. That is why we must be Catholic Radicals; we must get down to the roots. That is what radicalism is—the word means getting down to the roots." Day recalled in a memorial issue of the *Catholic Worker* years later that

> Peter, even in his practicality, tried to deal with problems in the spirit of "the Prophets of Israel and the Fathers of the Church." He saw what the Industrial Revolution had done to human beings and he did not think that unions and organizations, strikes for higher wages and shorter hours, were going to be the solution. "Strikes don't strike me," he used to say when we went out to a picket line to distribute literature during a strike. But he came with us to hand out the literature—leaflets which dealt with men and women's dignity and their need and right to associate themselves with their fellows in trade unions, in credit unions, cooperatives, maternity guilds, etc. He never preached; he taught. While

decrying secularism, the separation of the material from the spiritual, his emphasis . . . was on our material needs, our need for work, food, clothing and shelter. Though Peter went weekly to confession and daily to Communion and spent an hour a day in the presence of the Blessed Sacrament, his study was of the material order around him. Though he lived in the city, he urged a return to the village economy, the study of the crafts and of agriculture. He was dealing with this world, in which God has placed us to work for a new heaven and a new earth "wherein justice dwelleth."[12]

For seventeen years, Peter continued to serve in the role of Day's mentor. Clearly she was in charge of leading and directing the *Catholic Worker* paper and the Catholic Worker movement, but she always felt grateful for his guidance of her vocation. In the last decade of his life, Maurin suffered a stroke and fell increasingly silent as his memory failed. He lamented that he could no longer think or recite his "Easy Essays." Day lamented that "he had given everything he had and he asked for nothing, least of all for success. He gave himself, and—at the end—God took from him the power to think." On May 15, 1949, he died at Maryfarm in Newburgh, New York. Garbed in a donated suit of clothes, he was buried in a donated grave in St. John Cemetery in Brooklyn. Obituaries appeared not only in the *Industrial Worker*, a radical labor paper on the government's subversive list, but also in *Osservatore Romano*, the Vatican's semiofficial newspaper, which announced Maurin's death on its front page.

The first issue of the *Catholic Worker* contained news of the exploitation of black Americans in the South, the abuses of child labor, and a local strike over wages and hours. The paper sold for a penny a copy, as it still does today. Day served as both editor and journalist. Her column "Day by Day," later retitled

"On Pilgrimage," constituted a running commentary on her travels, reporting on daily life in Catholic Worker houses in New York and elsewhere, reflections on books she was reading, and comments about national and world events, much of it taken from her journals, written in a lively, anecdotal, participatory style, yet leavened with biting criticism of injustice along with appeals to morally and religiously based arguments. The pages were illustrated—with wood-carved prints of favored saints by Ade Bethune, Fritz Eichenberg, and other contemporary artists.

"There was no formal 'rule' to life in a CW house. Dorothy likened it to a family. And over this sometimes fractious family Dorothy was the unquestioned matriarch."[13] At the heart of the houses was the virtue of hospitality. The Catholic Worker movement would succeed

> when (she remarked) we succeed in persuading our readers to take the homeless into their homes, having a Christ room in the house as St. Jerome said, then we will be known as Christian because of the way we love one another. We should have hospices in all the poor parishes. We should have coffee lines to take care of the transients; we should have this help we give sweetened by mutual forbearance and Christian Charity. But we need more Christian homes where the poor are sheltered and cared for. . . . So we do not cease to urge more personal responsibility on the part of those readers who can help in this way. Too often we are afraid of the poor or the worker. We do not realize that we know him and Christ through him, in the breaking of the bread.[14]

The historic precedent for this hospitality, according to Maurin, lay in "the fourteenth statute of the so-called council of Carthage, held about 436, [which] enjoins upon the Bishops to have hospices or houses of hospitality in connection with their churches. Today we need houses of hospitality as much as they needed them then. . . . We have parish houses for the priest, parish houses for educational purposes, parish houses for recreational purposes, but no parish houses of hospitality."[15]

In her Christmas essay for the December1945 issue of the *Catholic Worker*, Day made explicit the religious core of the movement's message:

> It is no use saying that we are born two thousand years too late to give room to Christ. . . . Christ is always with us, always asking for room in our hearts. . . . And giving shelter or food to anyone who asks for it, or needs it, is giving it to Christ. . . . If we hadn't got Christ's own words for it, it would seem raving lunacy to believe that if I offer a bed and food and hospitality to some man or woman or child, I am replaying the part of Lazarus or Martha or Mary, and that my guest is Christ. There is nothing to show it, perhaps. There are no halos already glowing round their heads—at least none that human eyes can see. . . . We are not born too late. We do it by seeing Christ and serving Christ in friends and strangers, in everyone we come in contact with. . . . He made heaven hinge on the way we act toward Him in His disguise of commonplace, frail, ordinary humanity.[16]

The houses of hospitality became centers for practicing the "Works of Mercy"—a program of action drawn from the twenty-fifth chapter of the Gospel of Matthew (verses 31–46) as the commandments by which all will be judged: to feed the hungry, give drink to the thirsty, clothe the naked, shelter the homeless, tend to the sick, visit the imprisoned, and bury the dead.

The ideal of farming communes fell far short of Maurin's vision of a back-to-the-land movement. Some were communal, in the sense that a few families owned them in common, but most were farms in little more than name, and were devoted primarily to taking in wayfarers as well as the sick and indigent from nearby cities. One big obstacle to the realizing of Maurin's dream was Day's insistence that need rather than efficiency as workers be the chief criterion in selecting guests. "We console ourselves . . . with the thought that, while we may not be establishing model communities, many a family is getting a vacation, many a sick person is being nursed back to health, crowds of slum children have the run of fields and woods for weeks, and groups of students spend happy hours discussing the Green Revolution."[17] Unfortunately, there was always a surplus of people who preferred a discussion of theology or politics to work on the fields or the repair of a hinge. "It seemed," Day noted, "that the more people there were around, the less got done."[18] Small matters took on divisive significance. Maurin alone seemed to look after basic chores. In 1944, part of the first farm in Easton, Pennsylvania, was sold, and another part was given away to a cantankerous group that regarded itself as "the true Catholic Workers." Other "farms" were set up, but were more rural houses of hospitality than agricultural communities.

A strong believer in education through dialogue, Maurin advocated "round table discussions for the clarification of thought," Friday night meetings that quickly became a tradition of the Catholic Worker community and attracted over the years the famous, such as Jacques Maritain, Robert Coles, and Michael Harrington, and the less famous, such as the author of this book.

The core Catholic Worker principles were three: voluntary poverty, personalism, and pacifism. Day captured her choice of personal poverty in a simple reflection on socks:

> I sit here [on a solitary day of recollection] on a clear cold winter's afternoon down on Long Island, surrounded by a snow-

covered countryside, and listen to the Philharmonic Symphony. At the same time I darn stockings, three pair, all I possess, heavy cotton, gray, tan, and one brown wool, and reflect that these came to me from the cancerous poor, entering a hospital to die. For ten years I have worn stockings which an old lady, a dear friend, who is spending her declining years in this hospital, has collected for me. . . . Often these have come to me soiled, or with that heavy, hospital smell which never seemed to leave them, even after many washings. . . . But the fact remains that I have stockings to cover me when others go cold and naked."[19]

In an editorial column, Day briefly summarized the communal poverty of the Catholic Worker movement:

We do not ask church or state for help, but we ask individuals, those who have subscribed to *The Catholic Worker* and so are evidently interested in what we are doing, presumably willing and able to help. Many a priest and bishop sends help year after year. Somehow the dollars that come in cover current bills, help us to catch up with payments on back debts, and make it possible for us to keep on going. There is never anything left over, and we always have a few debts to keep us worrying, to make us more like the very poor we are trying to help.[20]

As scholar Mel Piehl observed in his perceptive analysis of the Catholic Worker, *Breaking Bread*: "Since the movement believed that the vows of poverty of many Catholic religious [orders] had been rendered meaningless by the collective wealth of their orders, the Workers took care that the group as a whole should not accumulate assets beyond the bare minimum. The movement, as well as its individual adherents, was to remain in a constant state of 'precarity,' which was described as 'the opposite of security.'" Rare surpluses were given away, and the Catholic Worker refused to incorporate as a tax-exempt charity. As Day put it, "One who has accepted hardship and poverty . . . lays himself open to this suscepti-bility to the sufferings of others."[21] Another core value of the Catholic Worker movement was "personalism," an emphasis not only on the value of each and every individual but also the responsibility of each person to do the works of mercy in "a hands-on way"—that is, to appreciate the needs of the poor through face-to-face contact instead of the institutionalized and depersonalized structures of charitable giving. A major criticism of the Catholic Worker was its failure to empha-size structural/institutional change. The Catholic Worker's defense was that institutional change cannot be uncoupled from the individual actions of particular people, through the witness of personal acts, including speaking, writing, and demonstrating to effect change in themselves and others. It is good to write a check, but it is as—if not more—important to demonstrate an act of tangible compassion by serving a bowl of soup to a hungry person with one's own hands. As Maurin put it, "We must have a sense of personal responsi-bility to take care of our own, and our neighbor, as a personal sacrifice. . . . That is a first principle. . . . Charity is personal. Charity is love."[22]

The *Catholic Worker* newspaper helped its readers to en-visage a historical heritage of compassionate sanctity avail-able and present through time and distance, both as exem-plary and intercessory: Saint Francis of Assisi's devotion to poverty, Saint Teresa of Avila's balance of activism and deep prayer, Saint John of the Cross's contemplative mysticism, Saint Catherine of Siena's combination of spirituality and public involvement in church and state affairs, Saint Thér-èse of Lisieux's "Little Way" of sanctity, the Desert Fathers' devotion to ascetic solitude, Saint Benedict Joseph Labre's wandering poverty, Saint Vincent de Paul's devotion to the poor, plus the modern example of Mahatma Gandhi, Martin Luther King Jr., and Cesar Chavez, with their religiously inflected activism. Stories about and images of these model figures studded the pages of the newspaper and the prayers of workers (and fellow travelers), who turned to these saints for intercession and assistance.

Moreover, the personalism of the Catholic Worker was rooted deeply in the Roman Catholic doctrine of the Mystical Body of Christ, based on the Pauline image of the Christian community as members of a body of which Christ is the head. This belief held that the church is the extension of Christ's physical and spiritual presence through time and history, linking Christians past and present in a bond of unity and interdependence. If one member of the body suffers, all suffer; if one member rejoices, all rejoice. The source of the ongoing life of the church as the Mystical Body is observance of the sacramental and liturgical practice of the church. Theology professor William Cavanaugh expressed this best when he observed,

> As Day wrote in 1940: "This work of ours toward a new heaven and a new earth shows a correlation between the material and the spiritual. . . . Hence the leaders of the work, and as many as we can induce to join us, must go daily to Mass, to receive food for the soul. It is Christ in the Eucharist who builds His Mystical Body; we can only witness to it in our action." In her view, the Mystical Body of Christ did not exist above history either as a purely interior spiritual experience or an experience of communion after death. The Mystical Body of Christ was a real, concrete communion of human bodies which directly challenged other, violent attempts to organize human bodies to do one another harm, specifically

the configuration of the nation-state. Dorothy Day refused to claim the soul for Christ and hand the body over to the state.[23]

In her own words, Day stated,

> We think of all men as our brothers then, as members of the Mystical Body of Christ. "We are all members, one of another," and, remembering this, we can never be indifferent to the social miseries and evils of the day. The dogma of the Mystical Body has tremendous social implications. All the work . . . against extreme nationalism, against racial hatreds, against social injustice has its basis in an understanding of the liturgical prayer of the Church and a participation in it. When we pray in this way we recognize the universality of the Church; we are praying with white and black men [and women] of all nationalities all over the world. We partake of the same food, Christ. We put off the old man and put on Christ. The same blood flows through our veins, Christ's. We are the same flesh, Christ's. But all men are members or potential members, as St. Augustine says, and there is no time with God, so who are we to know the degree of separation between us and the Communist, the unbaptized, the God-hater, who may tomorrow, like St. Paul, love Christ.[24]

For this reason, it was common for Catholic Worker house members and volunteers to pray some of the monastic hours of the day. She explained "that living the liturgical day as much as we are able, beginning with prime (in the morning), using the missal for Mass, ending the day with compline and so going through the liturgical year we find that it is now not us, but Christ in us, who is working to combat injustice and oppression. We are on our way to becoming 'other Christs.'"

Personalism also led Day and Maurin to advocate for an economic and political order that would support the personal dignity of each person in the form of distributism and anarchism. To defuse the animus aroused by these two terms, Day wrote in the November 1957 issue of the *Catholic Worker*,

> Every House of Hospitality is a family with its faults and vir-
> tues, and above all, its love. We can all look at each other and
> say, we are all members one of another, since all are mem-
> bers or potential members of the Body of Christ. Even those
> dread words, *pacifism and anarchism*, when you get down to
> it means that we try always to love, rather than coerce, to be
> what we want the other fellow to be, to be the least, to have
> no authority over others, to begin with that microcosm man,
> or rather ourselves.

Independently, Day and Maurin had both been influenced by reading the works of Kropotkin, the Russian proponent of cooperative forms of labor, with workers sharing fairly in profits and the ownership of the means of capital. They also read and quoted the works of the English Catholic dis-tributists, G. K. Chesterton, Hilaire Belloc, Eric Gill, and Father Vincent McNabb, whose views were more in line with papal teaching on just economy with its emphasis on the principle of subsidiarity. According to the social teaching of Pius XI in *Quadragesimo Anno* (1931), reinforcing that of Leo XIII in *Rerum Novarum* (1891), governments should undertake only those initiatives that exceed the capacity of individuals or private groups to achieve. Observing this prin-ciple would safeguard the personal responsibility and free-dom of persons and small communities. As the latter-day en-vironmentalist and personalist, E. F. Schumacher famously put it, "Small Is Beautiful." Anarchism, for Day and Maurin, meant suspicion of the tendency of the nation-state, whether capitalist or Communist, to centralize power in bureaucratic structures that, in effect, render the person powerless. As a consequence of this distrust, Day never voted.

Pacifism has been the most controversial commitment of the Catholic Worker movement. When the Spanish Civil War broke out in 1936, most American Catholics supported Francisco Franco, but the *Catholic Worker* declared itself neutral: "We are not praying for victory for Franco. . . . Nor are we praying for victory for the loyalists whose . . . leaders are trying to destroy religion. We are praying for the Spanish people—all of them our brothers in Christ—all of them Temples of the Holy Ghost, all of them members or potential members of the Mystical Body of Christ." This stance of neutrality troubled some members of the Catholic hierarchy and laity, and lost the Catholic Worker support as some parishes canceled bulk subscriptions to the newspaper. Nevertheless, Day maintained a pacifist stance on the advent of the Second World War. The June 1940 editorial "Our Stand" declared, "For eight years we have been opposing the use of force—in the labor movement, in the class struggle, as well as in the struggles between countries. . . . But we consider that we have inherited the Beatitude ('Blessed are the peacemakers') and that our duty is clear."[25] As a consequence of her persistent pacifism, there was a drop in the paper's circulation, dissension in the houses, and a mountain of angry letters. When the United States entered the war in 1941, Day continued to urge pacifism. There were reductions in the number of houses due to lack of staff and drop-off of unemployed men due to the draft. Maurin advised her that "perhaps silence would be better for a time than to continue our opposition to war. Men are not ready to listen." She refused to give in. And as she later noted, "Although we opposed the war and upheld the stand of the conscientious objector and the absolutist who advocated nonpayment of taxes and non-registration, we were able to continue and there was no attempt . . . to suppress us."[26] The FBI, however, had been watching her even before the war. And J. Edgar Hoover confidentially recommended placing her in custodial detention in the event of a national emergency.

The plight of those who were detained during the war aroused Day to visit Japanese internment camps on the West Coast and describe the experience in the June 1942 issue of the *Catholic Worker*:

> I saw a bit of Germany on the west coast. I saw some of the concentration camps where the Japanese men, women and children are being held before they are resettled in the Owens Valley or some other place barren, windswept, inaccessible. The strange part of this wholesale imprisonment of an innocent people is that many of them are native born citizens of this country. But that means nothing in wartime. Wholesale evacuation of areas in Los Angeles, San Francisco, Portland and Seattle has already been carried out and as I stopped in each city, there were still groups being moved. Whole areas had been vacated, houses empty. According to friends in Portland, business and property had to be sold at a loss and there were those who took advantage of this misfortune of the evacuees. I have read a number of letters from Japanese girls to school mates, from mothers of families to friends of ours. All speak of bitter misery and bewilderment.

Day protested bitterly against the bombing of Hiroshima and Nagasaki, and observed its anniversary as a day of fast and penance for what she saw as an overwhelming atrocity. As did Ammon Hennacy, a prominent Catholic Worker activist, who for years publicly protested with placards and urged passersby to join him. Each year he added a day to his fast to observe the date, August 5. On that day in 1956, Day joined with A. J. Muste, and Bayard Rustin in delivering a letter to the office of the Japanese embassy expressing sorrow for the destruction of Hiroshima and Nagasaki.[27] In the 1950s, Day joined public demonstrations against compulsory air raid drills, arguing that there was no safety against atomic weapons, and was jailed and fined for noncompliance several times. She voiced strong opposition to the Vietnam War, and joined Muste in encouraging young men to resist conscription and burn their draft cards publicly. She had read about the French colonization of Vietnam through her devotion to Saint Thérèse of Lisieux, who corresponded with Father Theophane Venard, a missionary to Indochina, who was critical of the French colonial regime. Day linked America's involvement in Vietnam to involvement in Latin America, and in the January 1967 issue of the *Catholic Worker*, she castigated US complicity with tyranny in other areas of the world:

> It is not just Vietnam, it is South Africa, it is Nigeria, the Congo, Indonesia, all of Latin America. It is not just the pictures of all the women and children who have been burnt alive in Vietnam, or the men who have been tortured, and died. It is not just the headless victim of the war in Colombia. It is not just the words of Cardinal Spellman. It is the fact that whether we like it or not, we are Americans. It is indeed our country, right or wrong, as the Cardinal said. . . . We are warm and fed and secure. . . . We are the nation the most powerful, the most armed and we are supplying arms and money to the rest of the world where we are not ourselves fighting. We are eating while there is famine in the world. . . . Woe to the rich! We are the rich. The works of mercy are the opposite of the works of war, feeding the hungry, sheltering the homeless, nursing the sick, visiting the prisoner. But we

are destroying crops, setting fire to entire villages and to the people in them. We are not performing the works of mercy but the works of war. We cannot repeat this enough.

The Catholic Worker supported antiwar activists, including Jim Forest, Daniel and Philip Berrigan, Thomas Merton, and other less prominent members of the Catholic peace movement. When Merton was forbidden by the father general of his order to publish any further books on issues of war and nuclear arms, the *Catholic Worker* published several of his antiwar essays under the none-too-subtle pseudonym of "Benedict Monk."

As noted above, Day's acts of civil disobedience brought her into contact with Muste. She had spoken several times at the Community Church at his invitation. On November 6, 1965, she appeared on stage at an open-air demonstration with him in support of five young men who were to burn their draft cards:

> I speak today as one who is old, and who must endorse the courage of the young who themselves are willing to give up their freedom. I speak as one who is old, and whose whole lifetime has seen the cruelty and hysteria of war in this last half century. . . . I wish to place myself beside A.J. Muste to show my solidarity of purpose with these young men, and to point out that we too are breaking the law, committing civil disobedience, in advocating and trying to encourage all those who are conscripted, to inform their consciences, to heed the still, small voice, and to refuse to participate in the immorality of war.

Meanwhile, counterdemonstrators on the other side of the square chanted "Moscow Mary! Give us joy. Bomb Hanoi!" and "Burn yourselves, not your cards!"[28]

In the arena of race relations, Day supported the Southern Tenant Farmers' Union in Arkansas. The terrible conditions under which the southern tenant farmer unionists lived and the violence that continually imperiled them prompted her to telegraph Eleanor Roosevelt, who responded at once with an appeal to the governor for an investigation. Day went to Americus, Georgia, in April 1957, to visit Koinonia Farm, founded by Baptist minister Clarence Jordan, as a racially integrated community. In the May issue of the *Catholic Worker*, she described a frightening experience:

> Last night I was shot at for the first time in my life. They sat up for fear of fires, and being short of manpower, Elizabeth and I watched from 12 to 3 A.M. she, with her accordion to while away the night watches with hymns, and me with my breviary, remembering the Trappists rising at two. Friday nights are bad nights, many cars passing. Usually we get out to let them see people are on hand. But this time, at one thirty, we were sitting in the first and second seats of a station wagon, under a flood light, under a huge oak tree, and a car slowed up as it passed and peppered the car with shot. We heard sounds of repeated shots . . . and we were too startled to duck our heads. I was shaken of course. There was no other sound from the slowed down car, which gathered speed and disappeared down the road. . . . I was shaking both from fright and the cold night air. We continued our watch until three but nothing else happened.[29]

She consistently supported the civil rights movement and defended King's doctrine of nonviolent protest. Day also spoke out on behalf of the struggle of the United Farm Workers led by Chavez, and was arrested and jailed for the last time in her life for trespassing in the grape fields of Delano Valley, California, in August 1973, at the age of seventy-six. Day had personally met Chavez when he visited the house on a trip to New York for a boycott demonstration. He was pleasantly surprised to see there an image of Our Lady of Guadalupe, patron of Mexico and the farmworker demonstrators, who carried her image at the front of their marches. From its first issue, the masthead of the *Catholic Worker* featured an African American, Indian, or Chicana worker grasping hands with a white worker beside the figure of Christ with a cross in the background.

Continuously aware of the stark realities of urban poverty, Day had little patience with romantic depictions of her charity. In response to a Catholic newspaper's expression of sympathy for the Catholic Worker's "sentimentality," Day replied in the February 1942 issue of the *Catholic Worker*, ending with the words of one of her favorite quotations:

> But let those who talk of softness, of sentimentality, come to live with us in cold, unheated houses in the slums. Let them come to live with the criminal, the unbalanced, the drunken, the degraded. . . . Let them live with rats, with vermin, bedbugs, roaches, lice. . . . Let their flesh be mortified by cold, by dirt, by vermin; let their eyes be mortified by the sight of bodily excretions, diseased limbs, eyes, noses, mouths. Let their noses be mortified by the smells of sewage, decay, and rotten flesh. Yes, and the smell of . . . sweat, blood, and tears. . . . Let their taste be mortified by the constant eating of insufficient food cooked in huge quantities for hundreds of people, the coarser foods, so that there will be enough to go around; and the smell of such cooking is often foul. Then, when they have lived with these comrades, with these sights and sounds, let our critics talk of sentimentality. As we have often quoted Dostoyevsky's Father Zosima, "Love in practice is a harsh and dreadful thing compared to love in dreams."

Her travels on behalf of the *Catholic Worker* were frequent, extensive, and exhausting. In the fall 1951 issue of the paper she wrote, "I have visited twenty-seven cities, from Fall River, Mass., to Fargo, North Dakota. I have been bone-tired and mind-tired. I have slept on buses and trains, on boards and beds, in rooms with babies, in dormitories, in solitary splendor. I have eaten in homes where elegance is the rule and at Houses of Hospitality with men from skid row."[30] On November 29, 1980, Day died quietly in her room at Maryhouse on Third Street in the Bowery. At her funeral, she was carried by her grandchildren in a plain, unvarnished pine coffin to the Church of the Nativity, half a block away. Among the mourners was Forster Batterham. As one of the mourners noted, "Nothing would have astonished her more than seeing him among those waiting in line to receive communion." One journalist asked Peggy Scherer, editor of the *Catholic Worker* at the time, whether the movement could continue without its founder. "We have lost Dorothy," she replied, "but we still have the Gospel." Day was buried at Resurrection Cemetery on Staten Island not far from the beach house where she had spent such significant years of her life. A small gravestone reads "DEO GRATIAS."

In 1997, then cardinal archbishop of New York, John Cardinal O'Connor, initiated the process of Day's canonization. In 2000, the Vatican approved her cause, and she is classed as "Servant of God," the first stage in canonization. In its August 27, 2001 issue, *America*, for which Day had written a number of articles over the years, assessed her significance in a memorial article, "Celebrating Dorothy Day": "Without dismissing the importance of other leaders in the history of the Roman Catholic Church in the United States, it is fair to say that Dorothy Day remains, at the dawn of the new millennium, the radical conscience of American Catholicism. [Her life was] a unique combination of social activism and deep religious feeling. The dual passion of social justice and intimacy with God was present in her life from early childhood." In their 1983 pastoral letter, *The Challenge of Peace*, the US bishops singled out Day, King, and Gandhi as major influences on the spread of nonviolent options to war and for having a profound impact on the life of the church in the United States in the twentieth century, and their 1986 pastoral letter, *Economic Justice for All*, placed renewed emphasis on the plight of the poor long preached by the Catholic Worker.

President Barack Obama in his book *The Audacity of Hope* (2006) includes Day in a list of "great reformers in American history" who were motivated by their faith and "repeatedly used religious language to argue their causes."[31] The others he mentioned were Frederick Douglass, Abraham Lincoln, Jane Addams, Abraham Joshua Heschel, and King. In his September 2015 address to the US Congress, Pope Francis included "the servant of God" Day along with Lincoln, King, and Merton as exemplary Americans for their dedication to social justice and the rights of persons (Day), liberty (Lincoln), liberty in plurality (King), and the capacity for dialogue and openness to God (Merton).

By 2015, according to the Catholic Worker Web site, there were 207 "Catholic Worker communities in the U.S. and 25 abroad . . . committed to nonviolence, voluntary poverty, prayer and hospitality for the homeless, exiled, hungry, and forsaken. Catholic workers continue to protest injustice, war, racism, and violence of all forms." Circulation of the *Catholic Worker* published in New York is, as mentioned above, approximately ninety thousand, still priced at a penny per copy.

And Catholic Worker houses in Los Angeles, Houston, Philadelphia, Washington, DC, and several other cities publish local *Catholic Worker* newspapers as well. Influenced by the Catholic Worker, non-Catholic houses, like the Presbyterian-affiliated Open Door in Atlanta, offer food and hospitality to the needy in urban locales.

Moreover, the Catholic Worker peace activism lived on in the Plowshares movement's demonstrations against nuclear missile sites. Many of the demonstrators, often elderly, entered the sites again and again to paint warheads with human blood and strike them with hammers in a symbolic attempt to turn these weapons of mass destruction into "plowshares" of peace. Some were recidivists, disregarding their multiple arrests and prison terms. Most were associated directly with Catholic Worker houses or had been influenced by Day's insistence on the moral imperative of disarmament—the difficult doctrine that had so disturbed me as a college freshman in 1961.[32]

Interviewers and commentators have offered a glimpse of Day's personality. William Miller, her official biographer, observed, for example, that "Dorothy had, as her mother had said, a 'presence' about her, a controlled strength, unobtrusive but still a force. Without ever betraying the ordinary and usually unpleasant marks of assertiveness, she had a 'take charge' approach to things, and such was her poise, intelligence, and acumen that people were convinced immediately of the honesty and integrity of this plain but well-spoken woman."[33] Day herself lamented, "So imprudent am I, so hasty in speech." Asked if she had any regrets gazing back over the difficulties in her life, she remarked, "For a woman who had known the joys of marriage, yes, it was hard. It was years before I awakened without that longing for a face pressed against my breast, an arm about my shoulder. The sense of loss was there. It was a price I had paid." Day added, "The only answer in this life, to the loneliness we are all bound to feel, is community. The living together, working together, sharing together, loving God and loving our brother, and living close to him in community so we can show our love for Him."[34]

Figure 4.1 Howard Thurman. Photo courtesy of Boston University
Photography.

CHAPTER 4

HOWARD THURMAN

IN SEARCH OF COMMON GROUND

I am an invisible man. No, I am not a spook like those who haunted Edgar Allan Poe; nor am I one of your Hollywood-movie ectoplasms. I am a man of substance, of flesh and bone, fiber and liquids—and I might even be said to possess a mind. I am invisible; understand, simply because people refuse to see me. Like the bodiless heads you see sometimes in circus sideshows, it is as though I have been surrounded by mirrors of hard, distorting glass. When they approach me they see only my surroundings, themselves, or figments of their imagination—indeed, everything and anything except me. Nor is my invisibility exactly a matter of a biochemical accident to my epidermis. That invisibility to which I refer occurs because of a peculiar disposition of the eyes of those with whom I come in contact. A matter of the construction of their *inner* eyes, those eyes with which they look through their physical eyes upon reality.

—Ralph Ellison, *Invisible Man*

DO WE KNOW EACH OTHER? Do we really know each other? Or are we black and white people a country of strangers? The ongoing issue of race in this country remains the paradigmatic test of civic community. Fifty years after the passage of the landmark Civil Rights and Voting Rights acts of the mid-1960s, we are still a segregated society, not de jure, but de facto. And that fact creates distrust, dissension, unease, and fundamental disagreement about the character of race relations in the nation—with black Americans expressing much more pessimism than white Americans about the present and future state of affairs. (Meanwhile, the condition of the black poor in the inner cities continues to be an obstinate block to opportunity and equal access for masses of black youths, especially young black males.)

To be sure, the two peoples, black and white, do meet; we meet in the workplace and, to some extent and in some places, the schools (although schools reflecting the pattern of residential separation continue to be largely segregated, with devastating effect, as author Jonathan Kozol demonstrates in *Savage Inequalities*, *Amazing Grace*, *Ordinary Resurrections*, and *Fire in the Ashes*). And so we remain separate; we do not know each other's lives, we do not hear each other's stories, and we do not worship in each other's churches. The churches—the major sources of values, ideals, symbols, and identity for much of this nation's history—have failed, with few exceptions, to sustain meaningful interracial community. Nor have the symbols and institutions of the civil religion of the nation succeeded in maintaining lasting interracial community.

There have been moments, two in particular, when it seemed as if powerful revival movements within Christianity might bridge the racial divide, and bring black and white Christians into a fellowship of aims and attitudes. Both occurred at the turn of centuries. The end of the eighteenth and the beginning of the nineteenth was a time of evangelical awakening, when the Methodists and Baptists briefly opened a door that seemed to reveal the possibility of equality and biracial fellowship. The antislavery witness of the Methodists and some Baptists in the 1770s; their willingness to permit black men to pray, exhort, and preach in public; and especially their willingness to ordain them to pastor—all verged on a gospel of equality. But this door to religious equality was rapidly slammed shut by the intransigence of slavery in the South and persistence of racism everywhere in the nation. And so black churches sprang up, where possible, and the "invisible institution" of the slaves developed so that the "real preaching" of authentic Christianity, uncompromised by the heresy of slavery and racism, could be heard and celebrated in the land.

A century later, the Holiness-Pentecostal movement seemed poised to develop a truly interracial Christianity. The great three-year-long Azusa Street revival, begun in Los Angeles in 1906, involved interracial leadership, and included the participation of Asian and Mexican as well as European and African Americans. Early Pentecostals understood the interracial character of their movement as a sign of its authenticity—a new Pentecostal outpouring of the Holy Spirit on diverse races as well as diverse tongues. For a time, black Pentecostal leaders ordained whites to the ministry and involved themselves in interracial revivals. But once again, race emerged to constrain the movement's flow and turn it aside into the old well-worn paths of discrimination.

Two mid-nineteenth- and mid-twentieth-century civil religion movements brought whites and blacks together to cooperate in the black freedom struggle: the antislavery movement of the 1830s, 1840s, and 1850s, and the civil rights movement of the 1950s and 1960s. Collaboration, cooperation, and fellowship characterized both of these movements, and yet the fit of interests and attitudes kept slipping as black antislavery activists became disillusioned with the patronizing attitudes of even the most outspoken white abolitionists, and a century later, white veterans of the civil rights campaigns felt rejected and deeply hurt at the turn toward separatism of some of their black colleagues in the late 1960s and 1970s.

Today, the question asked by the Kerner Commission in 1967 remains a perennial one, still awaiting an answer. Are we two nations, or one? A visionary, prophetic voice attempted to bring this issue to the fore of the national consciousness and conscience. He not only described a vision of interracial religious community; he succeeded in creating it. In looking at the life and thought of this mystic, poet, ecumenist, and preacher, Howard Thurman, perhaps we may gain a measure of hope and wisdom for our own situation, if we, like him, are truly committed to the search for common ground.[1]

Thurman was born November 18, 1899, in West Palm Beach, Florida, and died in 1981 in San Francisco (from one ocean to the other bounding the continental United States— the ocean that brought his slave ancestors in the Middle Passage to the ocean that faced Asia and the Pacific Rim). His life span of eighty-one years witnessed a sea change in the conditions of black people in this country. Race relations in the years surrounding Thurman's birth have led historians to call the period from 1877 to 1918 the "nadir"—with good cause. Forty years after slavery, the erosion of the civil rights obtained during Reconstruction; disfranchisement of black southerners by intimidation, violence, and legal subterfuge; spread of Jim Crow laws across the South; the *Plessy v. Ferguson* Supreme Court decision that rendered the principle of "separate but equal" the law of the land four years before Thurman's birth; depiction of black people by popular culture and new pseudoscientific racial theories as a beast or, alternately, a child; gruesome accounts of mounting incidents of lynching—all seemed to demonstrate that race relations were getting worse, not better, as a new century dawned. Thurman was born into a society structured by rigid rules of segregation, a society in which a black person could never be sure when and where they might have to face humiliation, if not outright violence.[2]

Raised in Daytona, Florida, Thurman was fortunate to have a strong, nurturing family. He grew up with the integrity of his personality supported by the loving care of his mother, Alice, and grandmother Nancy Ambrose, both sensitive to his intellectual and spiritual gifts. He experienced the additional support of the Mount Bethel Baptist Church congregation and wider black community of his neighborhood as well. His grandmother Nancy, a former slave and a woman to be reckoned with, took Howard and other neighborhood black children in charge whenever she felt that their self-esteem had been damaged by the racism that circumscribed their young lives. She would gather them and repeat the story of an old slave preacher who was allowed to hold prayer meetings on her plantation during the closing years of slavery. After preaching a lengthy and emotionally exhausting sermon, he would always conclude, she remembered, by gazing intently into the face of each member of his slave congregation, and with as much forcefulness as he could muster, told them, "Remember, you aren't slaves; you aren't niggers; you are God's children."[3] Early on, Thurman derived from African American religion a sense of self-worth and affirmation.

During his childhood, Thurman also experienced a profound mystical intuition into the unity of all being, which provided a lasting touchstone for his vision of community. As he remembered it much later,

> As a boy in Florida, I walked along the beach of the Atlantic in the quiet stillness that can only be completely felt when the murmur of the ocean is stilled and the tides move

stealthily along the shore. I held my breath against the night and watched the stars etch their brightness on the face of the darkened canopy of the heavens. I had the sense that all things, the sand, the sea, the stars, the night, and I were *one* lung through which all of life breathed. Not only was I aware of a vast rhythm enveloping all, but I was a part of it and it was a part of me.[4]

He recognized this experience as one of the primary, defining moments of his life. Thurman does not identify the cultural antecedents to his experience, but the African American religious tradition, both in its folk (extra-ecclesial) and ecclesial dimensions, supported an intuitive understanding of the unity of all created being. Individual black folk artists have depicted such integral spiritual visions in paintings, sculptures, and mixed medias. And in the narratives of their conversion experiences, generations of black Christians typically spoke of arriving at an ecstatic state that filled them with an intense love for everything and everybody.

With assistance from local whites and blacks, Thurman went to the First Baptist Academy in Jacksonville for high school, since at that time there were only three public high schools for black children in the entire state of Florida. In 1919, he entered Morehouse College. (Martin Luther King Sr. was a fellow student, though in a different class.) There he encountered Benjamin Mays and John Hope, who exemplified for him and generations of black students the finest qualities of black intellectual and socially engaged leadership.

In his sophomore year, he joined the Fellowship of Reconciliation (FOR), where he "found a place to stand in my own spirit—a place so profoundly affirming that I was strengthened by a sense of immunity to the assaults of the white world of Atlanta, Georgia."[5] In his senior year, he applied to

the Newton Theological Seminary in Newton, Massachusetts, an institution he had read about from high school days.
He received a letter from the seminary's president expressing
regret that the school did not admit black men and referring
him to a southern black seminary, Virginia Union, where he
would be able to secure the kind of training he would need to
provide religious leadership for his people.

In 1926, Thurman applied to Rochester Theological Seminary (now Colgate Rochester Crozer Divinity School) in Rochester, New York. He knew that it was the seminary administra-
tion's policy to accept two and only two black students at the
same time. A number of racial incidents at Rochester alternately
amused, hurt, and angered him, but he persevered, and succeeded. On graduation, Thurman accepted his first call to
serve as a pastor of a black Baptist congregation in Oberlin,
Ohio. Shortly before assuming his pastorate, he married Katie
Laura Kelley, a graduate of Spellman who had studied at the
University of Chicago Divinity School before turning to social work in Atlanta. There she worked on the eradication
of tuberculosis in poor neighborhoods and, as it turned out,
contracted the disease herself. His preaching at Mount Zion
Baptist Church quickly began to attract a steady stream of
white visitors, Oberlin professors, students, and a mixed congregation of auditors, as the whites did not become members.
At this point, Thurman decided that he needed to cultivate
an inner life of prayer and meditation, hoping to connect his
needs on an experiential level with those of his congregation. One Sunday an incident occurred that revealed to him
the possibilities of the way he had intuitively stumbled on.
A Chinese Buddhist, who had attended Thurman's church
Sunday after Sunday, came to say good-bye: "When I close
my eyes and listen with my spirit I am in my Buddhist temple experiencing the renewing of my own spirit."[6] Thurman

sensed that barriers were crumbling, that he was breaking new ground.

Returning to the South in 1927, partly on the advice of Katie's doctor, Thurman took up a position as a professor of religion and the director of religious life at Morehouse and Spelman colleges. There Katie gave birth to their daughter, named Olive, after Olive Schreiner, the South African author, whose poetic sensibility resonated deeply with Thurman's. In spring term 1929, Thurman took a leave of absence from his pastoral and teaching duties to begin a program of independent study at Haverford College with the Quaker teacher and mystic Rufus Jones. With Jones, Thurman read widely on Christian mysticism and developed a special interest in two figures, Meister Eckhart and Saint Francis of Assisi. Thurman's own mystical experience resonated with Eckhart's idea of a still point at the heart of each person as the presence of God within and also with the Dominican preacher's emphasis on God as the ground of all being. And he found in the nature mysticism of Francis, with its profound compassion for all of God's creatures, a spirit akin to his own love of the environment in all its variety of fauna and flora. Jones's influence on Thurman proved to be formative, as it had on A. J. Muste, in helping him to connect the inner life of spirituality with the outer life of social reform. In December 1930, Katie, whose health had been steadily declining, died in Atlanta. Deeply depressed, Thurman took a leave of absence from teaching and traveled to Europe to recover in the anonymity of London, and the spectacular beauty of Switzerland and Scotland. He returned to his classes in Atlanta for fall 1931.

In June 1932, he married Sue Bailey, a former music teacher at the Hampton Institute who had been selected as the national secretary for the YWCA, and was a well-known speaker and ecumenical activist in her own right. By the time of the wedding, Thurman's career took a new and significant turn as he had accepted an offer from then Howard University president Mordecai Johnson to teach in the School of Divinity and serve as dean of the Andrew Rankin Memorial Chapel. From this position, Thurman extended his national reputation as a preacher and teacher of extraordinary talent and sensitivity.

Three years later, Howard and Sue Bailey Thurman accepted an invitation to travel with a "Negro delegation" to Ceylon, India, and Burma on a goodwill tour sponsored by the local Student Christian Movement. The trip included another couple, United Methodist pastor Edward Carroll and his wife, Phenola. The exhausting six-month journey turned out to be a catalyst for the Thurmans' future. After Thurman's first lecture, at the law club of the University of Ceylon, a young lawyer challenged his views on religion and race, asking one of those questions that haunts a person for years. Thurman recorded their exchange in his journal:

> "What are you doing here? This is what I mean—Africans were taken to America as slaves, by Christians. They were sold in America to other Christians. They were held in slavery for 300 years by Christians. They were freed as a result of economic forces rather than Christian idealism . . . and I understand that you are lynched in America by Christians. In light of all this, I think that for a young intelligent Negro such as you to be over here in the interest of a Christian enterprise is for you to be a traitor to all the darker peoples of the earth. Such I consider you to be. Will you please account for yourself and your very unfortunate position? How can you be a Christian after all that Christians have done to your people for centuries and continue to do to them today?"

Yes—Let me thank you for what you have said. Particularly am I deeply moved by your frankness, it is an excellent measure of your confidence in me. I am not here to bolster up a declining or disgraced Christian faith in your midst. I do not come to make converts of Christianity nor do I come as exhibit A as to what Christianity has done for me and my people. I am Christian because I think that the religion of Jesus in its true genius offers me very many ways out of the world's disorders. But I make a careful distinction between Christianity and the religion of Jesus. In my opinion the churches and all so-called Christian institutions are built prevail [prevalently?] upon the assumption that the strong man is superior to the weak man and as such the sound right to exploit the weak and be served by him. I am dead [set] against most of the institutional religion with which I am acquainted. I belong to a small minority of Christians who believe that society has to be completely reorganized in a very definite egalitarian sense, if life is to be made livable for the most of mankind. To us Christianity was a way out, originally, for an underprivileged minority in the Greco Roman Empire and became a world religion officially under a banner other than the banner of Jesus Christ. Finally I admit even more relative to slavery and Christianity than you indict but I see also that in all of this practice not one time was there an appeal to the central teaching of Jesus to bolster up the existing order. The work of the minority in America interested as I am in changing society is just as much a fact as the iniquity of the majority.[7]

Apparently satisfied with Thurman's reply, the lawyer responded, "Thank you Doctor. I feel much better relative to it all and I hope to come to see you again before you leave."[8]

Thurman's answer, elaborated most fully in his classic texts *Jesus and the Disinherited* (1949) and *The Luminous Darkness*

(1965), distinguished between Christianity, with its history of discrimination and prejudice, and the religion of Jesus, which supported the needs and demands of the disinherited. Black Americans, he argued, had recognized the religion of Jesus in the Christianity presented to them and had appropriated it as their own. In effect he claimed, "By some amazing gift of spiritual creativity, the slave undertook to redeem the religion the master had profaned in his midst." Thurman contended that Jesus had been a member of an oppressed and rejected minority. And he offered and continues to offer to those who suffer the realization that they are of infinite value as children of God. Moreover, the test of any religion "turns on what word" it has "to share about God with men who are the disinherited, the outsiders, the fringe dwellers removed from the citadels of power and control in the society."[9]

While in India, the Thurmans met with the poet Rabindranath Tagore and Kshitimohan Sen, a scholar of Indian religions with whom Thurman shared

> the most primary naked fusing of total religious experience with another human being of which I have ever been capable. It was as if we had stepped out of social, political, [and] cultural frames of reference, and allowed two human spirits to unite on a ground of reality that was unmarked by separateness and differences. This was a watershed of experience in my life. We had become a part of each other even as we remained essentially individual. I was able to stand secure in my place and enter into his place without diminishing myself or threatening him.[10]

The Thurmans were the first African Americans to meet with Mahatma Gandhi, who questioned them closely in a two-hour conversation about the history and current situation of the racial discrimination dividing white and black

Americans. At one point in their meeting, Sue led the others in the delegation in singing two well-known spirituals, "Were You There When They Crucified My Lord?" and "We Are Climbing Jacob's Ladder," while Gandhi and his assistants bowed their heads in prayer. Years later, Thurman recalled that Gandhi especially admired the first spiritual, because "it got at the root experience of the entire human race under the spread of the healing wings of suffering."[11] Thurman himself would reflect on the transcultural appeal of the spirituals in his books *Deep River* (1945) and *The Negro Spiritual Speaks of Life and Death* (1947). At the end of their conversation, Gandhi remarked that "it may be through the Negroes that the unadulterated message of nonviolence will be delivered to the world."[12]

Above all the experience of India pushed the couple toward a deeper and clearer perception of the interrelatedness of all people:

> We saw clearly what we must do somehow when we returned to America. We knew that we must test whether a religious fellowship could be developed in America that was capable of cutting across all racial barriers, with a carry-over into the common life, a fellowship that would alter the behavior patterns of those involved. It became imperative now to find out if experiences of spiritual unity among people could be more compelling than the experiences which divide them.[13]

It would take several years for this impulse to take tangible form, but it seemed clear that the Indian journey had crystallized for Thurman ideas and experiences that had been developing since childhood. Back at Howard, he received a letter forwarded to him by Muste. Thurman had served as one of three vice chairs of the FOR since 1940 and was well known by Muste. It was a letter of inquiry from Alfred Fisk, a white Presbyterian minister in San Francisco. Fisk, a philosophy professor at San Francisco State University, was searching for a black ministerial student or recently ordained black minister to take a part-time position as copastor of a church in a black neighborhood in San Francisco. Thurman had no candidate to suggest until he began to consider that the letter might be a call to him personally. Taking leave of his position at Howard, he and his family faced the pressing questions posed by the university's president: "How can you support your family? How will you manage? How will you live?" To which he responded, "I don't know, I don't know. All I know is God will take care of us."[14] To start on such a venture in 1944 did indeed require a leap of faith. American society was unthinkingly and unapologetically segregated; discrimination prevailed in housing, schools, labor unions, the armed forces, and churches. Nonetheless, Fisk and Thurman, white Presbyterian and black Baptist, became cofounders and copastors of the Church for the Fellowship of All Peoples—the only integrated church in both leadership and membership in the country. The church, significantly, first met in the house of a Japanese family vacated by their forced internment during World War II in a "relocation" camp. For the next nine years, Thurman worked to create a new kind of community, committed to the ideal that "religious experience must unite rather than divide men. There must be made available experiences by which the sense of separateness will be transcended and unity expressed—experiences that are deeper than all diversity but at same time are enriched by diversity."[15]

The congregation's worship and general church life concentrated on celebrating the variety of cultures represented in the membership, with a special focus on educating the children about each other's ethnic and cultural backgrounds through a summer camp run by the church. Thurman experimented with the Sunday service, incorporating a weekly period of guided meditation and reflective silence, influenced perhaps by Quaker practice by way of Jones. Deciding to become independent rather than placing itself under the authority of any one denomination, whose doctrinal definitions might restrict the church's ideal of inclusive fellowship, the congregation developed a statement of commitment to which all members pledged themselves. A nationwide network of affiliate or associate members was formed from visitors and supporters of the Church of the Fellowship's ideal. Thurman traveled extensively, lecturing and preaching to support the church as well as spread news of its mission. He was a mesmerizing preacher whose voice and presence articulated with power his vision of interracial religious community. Many of these sermons and meditations formed the basis for his books, including the volume *The Search for Common Ground* (1973), whose title I've used for this chapter.

After nine years in San Francisco, Thurman accepted a call to Boston University as dean of Marsh Chapel, where he continued to work to build community until his retirement in 1965. Returning to San Francisco, he chaired the Howard Thurman Educational Trust, a charitable and educational foundation, until his death in 1981.

At the time of his death, Thurman's institutional legacy consisted in the Church for the Fellowship of All Peoples, which continues down to the present day, and the Educational Trust, which gained scholarship assistance for needy students, assisted in a variety of educational and religious causes, and distributed Thurman's books and tapes of his sermons to a worldwide audience. Admirers of Thurman established over one hundred Thurman listening rooms in the United States, Asia, Africa, and Europe to disseminate his message. During his lifetime and since his death, the form and effectiveness of Thurman's influence on the social and political movements of his day have puzzled observers of his life. Some critics questioned the liberal character of his theology and his privileging of religious experience over doctrinal formulations. Traditionalists also criticized the boldness of his ecumenical liturgical experiments at Howard's Andrew Rankin Memorial Chapel and the Church of the Fellowship. Others felt disappointed that he did not emerge as a leader in the style of a Martin Luther King Jr. or a Gandhi. Thurman himself was well aware of this criticism and delighted in commenting on it by repeating a story related to him by Reinhold Niebuhr. Niebuhr, as the story went, had mentioned Thurman's name in a lecture one day, and a black student had responded, "I'm glad you mentioned that man. He is the great betrayer of us all. We were sure that he had the makings of a Moses and then he turned mystic on us." Thurman chose instead to exercise leadership behind the scenes by force of his personal presence and pastoral counsel. He served, for example, on the boards of several major "movement" organizations, including the FOR, Congress of Racial Equality, and National Association for the Advancement of Colored People. He acted as a regular adviser for more visible leaders of the civil rights movement, such as James Farmer, Bayard Rustin, Vernon Jordan, and King. When asked point-blank why he, himself, had not led a movement for nonviolent change in American society, Thurman replied, "I have never considered myself any kind of leader. . . . I'm not a movement man. It's not my way. I work at giving witness in the external aspect of my life to my experience of the truth. That's my way—the way the grain in my wood moves. I don't prescribe for anybody else, and I'm willing to make available any resources I have to help people who have other ideas. But I have to follow my way, because it's the only thing I have to respect."[16]

Influence is a difficult thing to measure. But an amazing number of people from varied religious, ethnic, and political backgrounds claim to have been affected by Thurman personally, or through his writings and taped sermons. Most of his books have been reprinted, and three of a series of four volumes of his papers have been published. Articles, dissertations, and monographs on aspects of Thurman's thought have mounted steadily since his death as new generations seek to discover the significance of Thurman for America's ongoing racial dilemma. As Thurman himself noted, that significance lies primarily in the authenticity of his own spiritual experience as powerfully conveyed to others through the mediation of the spoken and written word. Thurman believed—as did three other activist contemplatives, Jones, Abraham Joshua Heschel, and Thomas Merton—that true social change needed to be grounded in spiritual experience, which Thurman described as "the conscious and direct exposure of the individual to God." Probably echoing Heschel, he declared that "religious experience in its profoundest dimension is the finding of man by God and the finding of God by man."[17] Like these other sharers of the divine pathos, he believed that "God is the God of history. He does not stand apart as some mighty spectator but is in the process and the facts, ever shaping them (in ways that we can understand and in ways beyond our powers to grasp) to ends that fulfill a great and good destiny for me. This is no idle or pious wish. Examine the past and behold the unfolding of the living process."[18]

Thurman's vision of community was based on his profound awareness of the interrelatedness of all created being.

As long as I can recall reacting to the experiences of life, I have observed in myself a tendency—even more, an inner demand—for "whole-making," a feel for a completion in and of things, for inclusive consummation. . . . Every human being needs and is deeply nourished by the feeling of being cared for, of being dealt with totally or completely. There is an inexhaustible assurance of well-being that floods the life when one is aware of being touched at a center in one's self that is beyond all good and evil, beyond all merit and de-merit. This is true without regard to culture, background, or condition. There is an insistent connection between the need for well-being and the elemental necessity in all forms of life to actualize its own potential and thus fulfill itself.[19]

Community, then, is the goal of life intended by life's author. Life, in all its forms, seeks to realize itself, and to realize itself consists in achieving inner and outer community.

In the widespread myths of creation and origin, Thurman observed, different human societies over the ages have expressed their longing for a lost communion within and without, with the self, the other, and the created world. Within the myths of origin something deep resides, a latent memory of the soul, a memory of a lost harmony, a reminder "that the intent of the Creator of life . . . is that men must live in harmony within themselves and with one another and perhaps with all of life." If accounts of the world's beginning reflect memories of a lost past, utopian stories and prophecies of a time to come, when the lion shall lay down with the lamb, when people shall live free of conflict and hatred, they project a profound "hope about the human situation and about the future."[20]

Both memory and hope, myths of origin and utopian prophecies, illustrate the drive within the person for what Thurman calls "whole making." "As long as I can recall reacting to the experiences of life, I have observed in myself . . . an inner demand . . . for 'whole making,' a feel for completion in and of things, for inclusive consummation. Experiences must somehow fit together; they must make sense to the mind." Thurman goes on to identify the intellectual drive for coherence and order with the demand of life for unity. "The tendency of the mind for whole-making or 'seeing whole,' for seeking harmony, for community, is rooted in the experience of the body that in turn is grounded in all life." Life, as it expresses itself in human consciousness, seeks wholeness, no less than when it expresses itself "instinctually in so-called subhuman forms of life."[21] So the human search for "making whole" stands on a continuum with the drive of life for community in all its myriad forms. We fail to see this interconnection at our own peril, Thurman warns.

> One of the deceptive aspects of mind in man is to give him the illusion of being distinct from and over against but not a part of nature. It is but a single leap thus to regard nature as being so completely other than himself that he may exploit it, plunder it, and rape it with impunity. . . . This we see all around us in the modern world. Our atmosphere is polluted, our streams are poisoned, our hills are denuded, wildlife is increasingly exterminated, while more and more man becomes an alien on the earth and a fouler of his own nest. The price that is being exacted for this is a deep sense of isolation of being rootless and a vagabond. Often I have surmised that this condition is more responsible for what seems to be the phenomenal increase in mental and emotional disturbances in modern life than the pressures—economic, social, and political—which abound on every hand. The collective

psyche shrieks with the agony that it feels as a part of the death cry of a pillaged nature.[22]

Note the radical connection that Thurman posits between the mental health or sickness of persons and the health or sickness of the environment. Thurman not only connects humans' psychic condition to the condition of the environment but also argues that there is an "affinity" between human consciousness and the many other forms of consciousness that surround us. The more aware we become of these other forms of consciousness, the more our own sense of self becomes enlarged, and the more all of life seems to be intimately a part of us and we a part of it. Here he has in mind the connection of consciousness between humans and animals. He recalled a childhood experience to illustrate the point. One day when he was a little boy, Thurman ran over to the house of a neighborhood playmate. As he was about to pass the front of his friend's house to run around back to the yard, he was halted by a knock at the front window. His friend's father was motioning him to come in by the front door. Inside, Thurman was led by the father to a side window and outside he saw his friend's baby sister, a child under two, sitting in the dirt of the yard holding a rattlesnake. She released the snake, and it would crawl away and then crawl back. She would pick it up and then put it down, and the snake would crawl away and then come back. Eventually she tired of the game, put the snake down, and crawled to the back steps, whereupon the snake crawled away. Clearly, the child and the snake were playing.[23]

Thurman posits a ground of unity between animals and humans that makes nonverbal communication between them possible. In this interspecies bonding, "The mind temporarily gives up its sense of individuality and drops back into an original creative continuum in which boundaries of the human self are temporarily transcended" and consciousness enlarged.[24] Communion between persons and animals is based on life seeking to realize itself in all its forms.

Finally, community between humans is the source of identity for each person because within each of us, according to Thurman, the inner law of life ineluctably searches for wholeness and fulfillment. The fact that persons "need to be loved, to be understood, to be cared for is the essential stuff of community."[25] The primary place of human community is the family. But the nation also constitutes a community, not only a community of rights and responsibilities, but also of rites or rituals of belonging. When minority groups, whether African Americans, Native Americans, Hispanic Americans, or Asian Americans, find themselves outside the national community, excluded by those who are within, their exclusion has a devastating effect both on them and the nation as a whole. "Wherever citizens are denied the freedom of access to the resources that make for a sense of belonging, a sense of being totally dealt with, the environment closes in around them," in Thurman's view, "resulting in the schizophrenic dilemma of being inside and outside at one and the same time. Or worse still, they are subject to the acute trauma of not knowing at any given moment whether they are outsiders or insiders."[26] Such a denial of access assails persons "at the very foundation of their sense of belonging," affecting what goes on even in the primary place of community, the family. They become "outsiders" living in the midst of "insiders." This denial of community cuts deeply into the total life of the state, creating a "condition of guilt in the general society that has to be absorbed in order to keep life tolerable within the body politic"—a kind of low-level infection that periodically breaks out in virulent reactions. Historically, in the United States, the drive for wholeness and community of black people has suffered sustained attack from the residual awareness "that always and under any and all circumstances" their lives "were utterly at the mercy of the white world."[27] This history of threatened and enacted racial violence against black persons has not been faced fully, Thurman wrote in 1973.

> The heartrending years when hundreds of Negroes were lynched, burned, and butchered by white men whose women and children were often special spectators of the inhuman ceremony are conveniently forgotten. It is scarcely remembered how long it took to pass anti-lynching legislation. The *bodies* of Negroes remember, and their psyches can never forget this vast desecration of personality. The boundaries of any sense of community, the effectiveness of one's life as a person, the breakdown of the instinctual tendency toward whole-making, the personality violence from aggression, thwarted and turned in on one's self . . . the guilt inspired by anonymous fears that live in the environment—these are some of the shadows, the unconscious reaction to which must be understood as we try to find community in the presence of the . . . confrontation facing American society.[28]

When discrimination and racism intervene to destroy community, the very thrust of life itself is frustrated. And just as any living organism when attacked will counteract in self-defense, so will a person (or persons) react if attacked by the destruction or denial of community. The move toward black separatism in the late 1960s and early 1970s was, according to Thurman, just such a stage of reaction. Eventually, however, the consciousness of racial separateness must be caught up in the realization of human community. Thurman had no doubts about his own black identity, and valued the history and culture of his people. But he was also certain of the common ground of the human spirit.

Thurman described the situation between the races forty-three years ago as a confrontation. We still face a confrontation insofar as we still fail to see each other face to face. Invisibility remains a quality of our inner eyes, the eyes with which we look out on reality, in the words of Ellison's novel *Invisible Man* that begin this chapter. Faces must be shown and must be seen before interracial community is possible. This confrontation—in the sense of face to face—without the masks of evasion, fear, discomfort, and false civility, must occur between white and black, painful and difficult though it may be, if we are to continue the search for common ground—the search that is the very manifestation of life within.

What if, down through the years, Thurman asked, in American life there had been imbedded in Christian orthodoxy a judgment that said that racial prejudice would bar a person from salvation? What if it had been taught and maintained all down the years that racial prejudice separates a Christian from God and his Christ? What might that have done for the search for common ground? What if today the churches, synagogues, mosques, temples, and—dare we hope—schools fostered the sustained confrontation (face to face) of black and white persons, not simply gathering together separately, but also letting the masks drop, telling their stories, and listening to one another—hard and frustrating, but necessary work.

In 1962, Thurman accepted an invitation to attend a lecture at a gathering of Canadian Indian leaders in Saskatchewan. As he was being introduced, he spontaneously decided to forego the use of a translator, despite objections that no one would be able to understand him. Perhaps he recalled his long ago experience with Sen in India.

At first the atmosphere was tense and disconcerting. It was quite clear that the men didn't understand my words and were puzzled by the unusual procedure. My words went forth, but they seemed to strike an invisible wall, only to fall back to meet other words flowing from my mouth. The tension was almost unbearable. Then, suddenly, as if by some kind of magic, the wall vanished and I had the experience of sensing an organic flow of meaning passing between them and me. It was as if together we had dropped into a continuum of communication that existed *a priori* long before human speech was formed into sounds and symbols. . . . When I finished, there was a long breath of silence as if together we were recovering our separate rhythms.[29]

Then, one by one, the Indian leaders approached him and repeated how each understood him as if he had spoken in their own language.

It is the possibility of such spiritual communication beyond, or rather beneath, differences of speech and culture that Thurman in his words and life insists we attend to:

I share with you the agony of your grief,
The anguish of your heart finds echo in my own.
I know I cannot enter all you feel
Nor bear with you the burden of your pain;
I can but offer what my love does give:
The strength of caring,
The warmth of one who seeks to understand
The silent storm-swept barrenness of so great a loss,
This I do in quiet ways,
That on your lonely path
You may not walk alone.[30]

Figure 5.1 "Official Portrait" of Thomas Merton (1963) by John Howard Griffin. Courtesy of the Estate of John Howard Griffin. John Howard Griffin Archive, Rare Book and Manuscript Library, Columbia University

CHAPTER 5

THOMAS MERTON

CONTEMPLATION IN A WORLD OF ACTION

> At the center of our being is a point of nothingness
> which is untouched by sin and by illusion, a point of
> pure truth, a point or spark which belongs entirely to
> God, which is never at our disposal, from which God
> disposes of our lives, which is inaccessible to the fan-
> tasies of our mind or the brutalities of our own will.
> This little point of nothingness and of absolute poverty
> is the pure glory of God in us. . . . It is like a pure dia-
> mond, blazing with the invisible light of heaven. It is
> in everybody, and if we could see it we would see these
> billion points of light coming together in the face and
> blaze of a sun that would make all the darkness and
> cruelty of life vanish completely.
> —Thomas Merton, *Conjectures of a
> Guilty Bystander*

THOMAS MERTON WAS BORN IN PRADES, FRANCE, IN 1915,
the son of Owen Merton, an artist from New Zealand, and
Ruth Jenkins Merton, an artist from the United States. His
mother died when Merton was only six, and his father when
he was fifteen. His childhood and adolescence were unset-
tled. Shuttling between France, England, Bermuda, and Long
Island, New York, Merton experienced the homelessness of

the expatriate, the rootlessness of the transient adrift in an uncaring world, and the longing of the orphan for family stability. Educated at European boarding schools, Cambridge University, and Columbia University between the two world wars, Merton also experienced the disillusionment with the modern world that many of the intellectuals of his generation felt. His conversion to Roman Catholicism incorporated him into a firmly established system of values and doctrines that countered the anomie and hedonism he deplored in modern society. "Leaving the world," he would find both a home and family in the community life of a Cistercian monastery in Kentucky.

Merton absorbed the temperament of the artist from his parents, although his talent expressed itself in writing instead of painting. This artistic perspective tended to nurture in him a critical distance from the world. Fortunately, Merton's superiors recognized and encouraged his vocation as a writer, and throughout his years in the monastery he remained an amazingly prolific author, publishing more than forty-eight books of poetry, essays, biography, autobiography, journals, meditations, and social criticism. Writing requires discipline and solitude. The strictly regulated life of a contemplative monk offered the disciplined structure Merton needed, and he himself helped persuade his order to recover the value of solitude in its own tradition by reinstituting the practice of allowing some monks to become hermits. He lived the last years of his life in a hermitage. Merton's distanced perspective on the world and need for disciplined solitude, derived from his expatriate past and sensibilities as a literary artist, were deepened, fulfilled, and—as we will see—transformed by the contemplative tradition in which he immersed himself.

There was in the young Merton the enthusiasm of the convert, which led him to espouse in his earlier works, like *The Seven Storey Mountain*, a world-rejecting attitude that he later came to recant: "The contemplative life is not," he wrote in 1964, "and cannot be, a mere withdrawal, a pure negation, a turning of one's back on the world with its suffering, its crises, its confusions and its errors. First of all, the attempt itself would be illusory. No man can withdraw completely from the society of his fellow men; and the monastic community is deeply implicated for better or worse, in the economic, political, and social structures of the contemporary world."[1]

We are all, according to Merton, in the fine phrase he used as the title of one of his published journals, "guilty bystanders." The Merton who had written a series of widely read modern spiritual classics—*Seeds of Contemplation* (1949), *The Ascent to Truth* (1951), *Bread in the Wilderness* (1953), *The Living Bread* (1956), and *Thoughts in Solitude* (1958)—was suddenly turning out volumes of essays on civil rights, nuclear weapons, and the Vietnam War, and expressing radical views on social and political issues. The Merton whose post–*Seven Storey Mountain* books on contemplation and monasticism had continued to attract a wide readership suddenly began to speak out forcefully on social issues: in 1961, on war and nonviolence, and in 1963, on civil rights and race. What, wondered many of his readers, did this new "turn toward the world" have to do with spirituality? Quite a lot, as one of his most perceptive interpreters argued:

> What had happened to him was that his solitude had issued into what all true solitude must eventually become: compassion. Finding God in his solitude, he found God's people, who are inseparable from God and who, at the deepest level of

their being (the level that only contemplation can reach), are at one with one another in God, the Hidden Ground of Love of all that is. This sense of compassion bred in solitude . . . moved him to look once again at the world he thought he had left irrevocably twenty years earlier . . . when he had entered the monastery. He now felt a duty, *precisely because he was a contemplative*, to speak out."[2]

This change was, no doubt, gradual, but Merton interpreted it in his journals as a revelatory experience. One of the most famous passages in Merton's writing, it is worth quoting extensively:

> In Louisville, at the corner of Fourth and Walnut, in the center of the shopping district, I was suddenly overwhelmed with the realization that I loved all these people, that they were mine and I theirs, that we could not be alien to one another even though we were total strangers. It was like waking from a dream of separateness of spurious self-isolation in a special world, the world of renunciation and supposed holiness. The whole illusion of a separate holy existence is a dream. Not that I question the reality of my vocation, or of my monastic life: but the conception of "separation from the world" that we have in the monastery too easily presents itself as a complete illusion: the illusion that by making vows we become a different species of being, pseudo-angels, "spiritual men," men of interior life, what have you. Certainly these traditional values are very real, but their reality is not of an order outside everyday existence in a contingent world, nor does it entitle one to despise the secular: though "out of the world" we are in the same world as everybody else, the world of the bomb, the world of race hatred, the world of technology, the world of mass media, big business, revolu-

tion, and all the rest. . . . This sense of liberation from an illusory difference was such a relief and such a joy to me that I almost laughed out loud. . . . To think that for sixteen or seventeen years I have been taking seriously this pure illusion that is implicit in so much of our monastic thinking. . . . I have the immense joy of being *man*, a member of a race in which God Himself became incarnate. As if the sorrows and stupidities of the human condition could overwhelm me, now I realize what we all are. And if only everybody could realize this! But it cannot be explained. There is no way of telling people that they are all walking around shining like the sun. This changes nothing in the sense and value of my solitude, for it is in fact the function of solitude to make one realize such things with a clarity that would be impossible to anyone completely immersed in the other cares, the other illusion, and all the automatisms of a tightly collective existence. My solitude, however, is not my own. It is because I am one with them that I owe it to them to be alone, and when I am alone they are not "they" but my own self. There are no strangers! *Then it was as if I suddenly saw the secret beauty of their hearts, the depths of their hearts where neither sin nor desire nor self-knowledge can reach, the core of their reality, the person that each one is in God's eyes.* If only they could see themselves as they really *are*. If only we could see each other that way all the time. There would be no more war, no more hatred, no more cruelty, no more greed. . . . But this cannot be *seen*, only believed and "understood" by a peculiar gift. . . . At the center of our being is a point of nothingness [Merton names it *le pointe vierge*] which is untouched by sin and by illusion, a point of pure truth, a point or spark which belongs entirely to God, which is never at our disposal, from which God disposes of our lives, which is inaccessible to the fantasies of our own mind or the brutalities of our will. This little point of nothingness and of *absolute poverty* is the pure glory of God in us. It is so to speak His name written in us, as our poverty, as our indigence, as our dependence, as our sonship. It is like a pure diamond, blazing with the invisible light of heaven. It is in everybody, and if we could see it we would see these billions of points of light coming together in the face and blaze of a sun that would make all the darkness and cruelty of life vanish completely. . . . I have no program for this seeing. It is only given. But the gate of heaven is everywhere.[3]

Note that Merton asserted that it was the particular task of the monk to speak out of his silence and solitude with an independent voice in order to clarify for those who were "completely immersed in other cares" the true value of the human person amid the illusion with which mass society surrounds the modern person at every turn. The contemplative then has a responsibility to dissent, lest by his forgetfulness, ignorance, and silence he actually complies with what he thinks he has left behind. Merton's turn to social criticism represents a *return* to concerns that he had before his entrance into the monastery.

His reflections on the nation's racial problem, for example, dated back at least to 1941, when he did volunteer work in central Harlem at Friendship House, a recreation program, clothing center, and library founded by the Baroness Catherine de Hueck (a friend of Dorothy Day). Impressed by her dedication to serving the poor, Merton seriously considered giving up his teaching position at St. Bonaventure College to join the staff at Friendship House full time. A retreat at the Trappist Abbey of Gethsemani in Kentucky, however, left Merton with a strong attraction for the monastic life. During fall 1941, three years after his conversion to Catholicism, he faced a difficult choice between the active life of serving the poor in Harlem and the contemplative life of ascetic silence and solitude at Gethsemani. In his journal entry for November 30, Merton attempted to clarify what attracted him to Harlem:

> A saintly woman in the tenements, was dying of cancer . . . but she was very holy and her holiness was in this suffering, and the Blessed Virgin has appeared to her. . . . There is no doubt that the Blessed Virgin Mary, when she appears to people in this country, appears in places like Harlem—or Gethsemani—are the stables of Bethlehem where Christ is born among the outcast and the poor. And where He is, we must also be. I know He is in Harlem, no doubt, and would gladly live where He is and serve Him there.

Merton was impressed not only by the poverty of Harlem but also by the mute judgment of its oppressed citizens against the degradation of the larger white society whose vices Harlem mirrored. He viewed both Harlem and Gethsemani as symbols of judgment as well as sites of holiness forestalling God's wrath against an evil society. On November 23, 1941, he attended a retreat for Friendship House volunteers led by Father Paul Hanley Furfey, a professor of sociology and social justice activist from Catholic University. Furfey's retreat focused on the Mystical Body of Christ, "the one infinite source of life," as Merton put it, "that nourishes both Friendship House and the Trappists." Merton claimed that he returned from the retreat "all on fire with it."[4] Perhaps we can catch a glimpse of Furfey's message from his book *Fire on the Earth*, published a few years before the retreat. Emphasizing the social implications of the doctrine of the Mystical Body, Furfey wrote,

If we realize that we are each bound to the other members of the human race in the Mystical Body of Christ, that we must love the human race as a whole, and love all the groups which constitute it, then we can scarcely fail to realize the evil as well as the stupidity of hating any part of the Mystical Body of Christ. . . . The same fact holds true in the field of race relations. There are persons who feel quite acutely the duty of individual kindness to persons of other races, and yet who seem to be totally unconscious of the injustice of race relations as a whole . . . who are violently antagonistic to any effort to reform the political, economic, social, and even religious oppression of the colored race. Would this be possible to anyone who really believed in the doctrine of the Mystical Body?[5]

In the end, Merton chose Gethsemani over Harlem, but he did not forget the racial issues that absorbed him in 1941.

During summer 1963, Merton wrote a series of three "Letters to a White Liberal." Revised and published in several journals, these letters formed a major part of *Seeds of Destruction*, published in 1964. The book attracted a good deal of critical attention, including a negative review in the *New York Herald Tribune* from University of Chicago historian of Christianity Martin Marty. Taking issue with Merton's criticism of white liberals and skepticism about the success of the civil rights movement, Marty accused the monk of posing as the white James Baldwin from behind the safety of his monastery's walls.

Marty and other critics were upset by Merton's accusation that white liberals were ignorant of and unprepared for the radical social change required to effectively solve America's race problem. White Americans were primarily interested in profits not persons. A truly radical reordering of priorities was needed. Once made aware of the cost of such change, white liberals would end up supporting the status quo. Addressing white liberals directly, Merton claimed that their participation in the March on Washington was not because blacks needed them but instead because they needed blacks. Actually, their participation blunted the revolutionary impact of the march. In plain and prophetically provocative language, Merton exposed the liberal's hypocrisy: "North or South, integration is always going to be not on our street but 'somewhere else.' That perhaps accounts for the extraordinary zeal with which the North insists upon integration in the South, while treating the Northern Negro as if he were invisible, and flatly refusing to let him take shape in full view, lest he demand the treatment due to a human person and a free citizen of this nation."[6]

Merton had indeed read Baldwin's *Nobody Knows My Name* (1961) and *The Fire Next Time* (1963), and agreed with his "statements about the futility and helplessness of white liberals, who sympathize but never do anything." Merton, now locating himself rhetorically alongside the liberal as a guilty bystander, observed that the "impotency is in our love of abstraction, our inability to connect with a valid image of reality. In a word, total alienation is the real tragedy, the real root of our helplessness. And our lotus-eating economy is responsible for that."[7] The roots of white racism were tangled up with the materialism, alienation, fear, and violence, spawned by a society bent on mindless, mass consumption. Consumerism commodified human relationships and trivialized freedom of choice, so that individuals became alienated not only from others but also from themselves. "Our trouble," Merton stated in *Seeds of Destruction*, is that we are alienated from our own personal reality, our true self. We do not believe in anything but money and the power of the enjoyment which comes from the possession of money."[8] The ironic tragedy of this condition is that the white man who thinks himself to be free "is actually the victim of the same servitudes which he has imposed on the Negro: passive subjection to the lotus-eating commercial society that he has tried to create for himself, and which is shot through with falsity and un-freedom from top to bottom. He makes a great deal of fuss about 'individual freedom' but one may ask if such freedom really exists. Is there really a genuine freedom for the person or only the irresponsibility of the atomized individual members of mass society?"[9] The alienation of the person from themselves, Merton insisted, led to violence: "The problem of racial conflict is part and parcel of the whole problem of human violence . . . all the way up from the suppressed inarticulate hate feelings of interpersonal family and job conflicts to the question of the H-bomb and mass extermination. The problem is in ourselves."[10]

In a direct letter to Baldwin, he acknowledged the power and truth of "The Fire Next Time" essays (which later became a book by the same name) when he read them in the *New Yorker*. "As I went through column after column I was struck, as I am sure you were, by ads all along each side of your text. What a commentary! They prove you more right than you could have imagined. They go far beyond anything you have said. What force they lend to all your statements. No one could have dreamed up more damning evidence to illustrate what you say."[11]

Merton was convinced that the alienation of the person from themselves is endemic to our society. One of the most consistent themes of his writing is the distinction between the true, or inner, self and the false, or external, self. We desperately need, Merton insisted, to move beyond our absorption in the false self to an awareness of the true self. "To have an identity is to be awake and aware," he wrote.

> But to be awake is to accept our vulnerability and death. Not out of stoicism or despair but for the sake of the invulnerable inner reality which we cannot recognize (which we can only be) but to which we awaken only when we see the unreality of our vulnerable shell. The only way to achieve this awareness is solitude, simplicity, and silence—the contemplative life. Not everyone can be a monk, but every Christian is called to develop within his or her life a dimension of silence and solitude in order to become aware of the inner self which is crucial in order to come to an awareness of God. Racism along with consumerism is only a symptom of alienation from the true self.[12]

Merton's pessimistic assessment, then, of the civil rights movement was due to his analysis of the need for profound social change, if the deep and tangled roots of the racial problem were ever to be addressed.

He agreed with white liberals that passing civil rights legislation was good and necessary, but also concluded that it was insufficient. How effectively and quickly would the laws be enacted on the local level? The resistance of southern whites to desegregation was backed with violence and seemed intransigent. In the North, "where such rights are still guaranteed in theory more than practice," civil rights legislation aroused "pressures and animosities" between whites and blacks. Merton noted perceptively that even if the law "were perfectly enforced it would still not be able to meet critical problems that were more strictly economic and sociological (jobs, housing, delinquency, irresponsible violence)." In short, he concluded, "Civil Rights legislation is not the end of the battle but only *the beginning of a new and more critical phase in the conflict.*"[13]

During this phase, Merton predicted, the paternalistic attitudes of white liberals would have to give way to a new modesty and respect for the independent leadership of blacks in the movement. White benevolence served as a mask for white leadership, and blacks readily saw it for what it was: an attempt to hold on to some control over the "Negro's fight for rights, in order to be able to apply the brakes when necessary." For the African American knows, Merton caustically observed, "that your material comforts, your security, and your congenial relations with the establishment are much more important to you than your rather volatile idealism, and that when the game gets rough you will be quick to see your own interests menaced by his demands. And you will sell him down the river for the five hundredth time in order to protect yourself."[14]

Merton firmly believed (as did A. J. Muste, Abraham Joshua Heschel, and Martin Luther King Jr.) that the civil rights movement was a *kairos* for the nation, a providentially appointed moment in history: "It is the Lord of History who demands of the Negro a complete break with his past servitudes. And the break must be made by the Negro himself without any need of the white man's paternalistic approval. It is absolutely necessary for the Negro to dissolve all bonds that hold him, like a navel cord, in passive dependence on the good pleasure of the white man's society."[15]

According to Merton, "One of the most striking and mysterious characteristics of the Negro freedom movement . . . is this sense, which awakening everywhere in the Negro masses of the South, especially in the youth, has brought them by the hundreds and thousands out of the ghettos," and "has moved them to action." Earlier than most, he understood the African American movement to be part of a larger worldwide movement by which "the entire Negro race and all the vast majority of 'Colored races' all over the world, have suddenly and spontaneously become conscious of their real power and . . . of a destiny that is all their own."[16]

But this destiny was not solely theirs *alone* . . . . "The white man, if he can possibly open the ears of his heart and listen intently enough to hear what the Negro is now hearing, can recognize that he is himself called to freedom and to salvation in the same *kairos* of events which he is now, in so many different ways, opposing or resisting."[17]

Why should the white man listen? Merton's answer to this question harks back to his youthful intuition of Harlem as a site of holiness and judgment. In a passage that rivals Baldwin for eloquence, Merton interpreted the profoundly religious meaning of the nonviolent civil rights movement to his white readers, many of whom had initially viewed it as a merely political conflict between extremist groups:

> The Negro children of Birmingham, who walked calmly up to the police dogs that lunged at them with a fury capable of tearing their small bodies to pieces, were not only confronting the truth in an exalted moment of faith, a providential *kairos*. They were also in their simplicity, bearing heroic Christian witness to the truth, for they were exposing their bodies to death in order to show God and man that they believed in the just rights of their people, knew that those rights had been unjustly, shamefully and systematically violated, and realized that the violation called for expiation and redemptive protest, because it was an offense against God and

His truth. They were stating clearly that the time had come where such violations could no longer be tolerated. These Negro followers of Dr. King are convinced that there is more at stake than civil rights. They believe that the survival of America is itself in question. . . . [They] are not simply judging the white man and rejecting him. On the contrary, they are seeking by Christian love and sacrifice to redeem him, to enlighten him, so as . . . to awaken his mind and his conscience, and stir him to initiate the reform and renewal which may still be capable of saving our society.[18]

In a lecture to the novices at Gethsemani, Merton discussed the ten-point pledge that the Birmingham marchers were asked to sign. The first four points included the promise to "meditate daily on the teaching and life of Jesus." Merton commented, "See, so that right away they sign up for a daily meditation." The pledge also urged people to "remember always that the nonviolent movement in Birmingham seeks justice and reconciliation not victory"; "this is putting it on a completely disinterested basis"; "to walk and talk in the manner of love, for God is love"; and "pray daily to be used by God in order that all men might be free." As Merton remarked, "Now, look at that. That's a terrific statement. It isn't just a question of 'pray that we may win,' or something like that, but pray and that's a very personal thing." Merton recommended that his students read the full ten-point pledge as a "monastic program" and asked them to ponder what it had in common with their monastic rule of life at Gethsemani.[19]

Clearly Merton had read and absorbed King's "Letter from Birmingham Jail." And he would himself memorialize the activists of Birmingham in poems on the child demonstrators, the death of Denise McNair, one of the four African American girls killed in the bombing of the 16th Street Baptist Church, and eventually the assassination of King. Merton deeply appreciated the religious motivation that moved the demonstrators to act:

> Such religion is not the "opium of the people," but a prophetic fire of love and courage, fanned by the breathing of the Spirit of God who speaks to the heart of His children in order to lead them out of bondage. Hence the numinous force . . . which makes itself felt . . . in the "Freedom Songs" which [the Negro] now sings, in the Baptist Churches of the South where he prepares to march out and face the police of states . . . which arm themselves against him with clubs, fire hoses, police dogs and electric cattle prods, throwing their jails wide-open to receive him. His song continues to resound in prison like the songs of Paul and his companions in the Acts of the Apostles.[20]

If whites chose not to listen to the message that blacks were trying to give America, Merton predicted at the end of his "Letters to a White Liberal" that "the merciful *kairos* of truth will turn into the dark hour of destruction and hate."[21]

On August 30, 1967, an open letter from Marty to Merton appeared in the *National Catholic Reporter*. Near the end of the "long hot Summer of Sixty Seven," Marty took the occasion to apologize for his negative 1963 review of Merton's *Seeds of Destruction*. Merton, he acknowledged, "told it like it is, and like it probably will be." In a letter dated September 6, 1967, Merton responded to Marty, pleased at the renewal of their friendship, but somber about the outbreak of racial riots around the country. "The injustice and cruelty which are by now endemic beneath the surface of our bland and seemingly benign society are too deep and too serious to be cured by legislation. . . . [The] un-Christianity of American

Christianity is going to be inexorably exposed and judged: mine perhaps, included." He suggested tentatively that "there is some hope that out of this hot summer we may at last get the serious beginning of a really effective radical coalition where, in spite of all the black separatism . . . there may in fact be collaboration between white and black on the left toward peace, new horizons of constructive change."[22] In the four years between Marty's review and his recantation, the momentum of the black liberation struggle seemed to have shifted from integration to black power, and from King's nonviolence to Malcolm X's "by any means necessary." Observing the rising tide of publicity around the Nation of Islam, Merton explained in a letter that

> it is understandable that they should now be taking the Muslim line more and more. After all, the Muslims have done more than anybody else to give them what a human being really needs: a chance to help himself and improve himself, an increase in self-respect and in the sense that his life has a meaning. What have the rest of us done in that way? The terrible thing about white liberalism has been its awful benevolence, the benevolence that assumes . . . that the Negro is utterly incapable of doing anything really significant for himself, and therefore that he is not fully human. I can see precisely why they are so mad.[23]

Responding to the new cries for black power, Merton took the militancy of H. Rap Brown and Stokely Carmichael seriously, refused to demonize them, and carefully explained the sources of their anger in the violence suffered by black people and their impatience at the slow pace of change. He wrote an appreciative review of Malcolm X's *Autobiography*, concluding that Malcolm was "a person whose struggles are understandable, whose errors we can condone. He was a fighter whose sincerity and courage we cannot help admiring, and who might have become a genuine revolutionary leader—with portentous effect in American society!"[24] He also widened his discussion of racism beyond the situation of African Americans to include Indians in North and South America as well as the cargo cults of Melanesia, noting their common experience of Western imperialism. "In one word, the ultimate violence which the American white man, like the European white man, has exerted in all unconscious 'good faith' upon the colored races of the earth (and above all on the Negro) has been to impose on them *invented identities*, to place them in positions of subservience and helplessness in which they themselves came to believe only in the identities which have been conferred upon them."[25]

In his last written statement on race, "From Nonviolence to Black Power," published in 1968 in *Faith and Violence*, Merton described his own role in the civil rights struggle: "The job of the white Christian is then partly a job of diagnosis and criticism, a prophetic task of finding and identifying the injustice which is the cause of *all* violence, both white and black, which is also the root of war."[26] Aware that the kairos moment of Christian nonviolence seemed to have passed, he did not despair but instead continued to hope for the realization of an earlier vision he had glimpsed many years before:

> A genuinely Catholic approach to the Negro would assume not only that the white and the Negro are essentially equal in dignity (and this, I think we do generally assume) but also that they are brothers in the fullest sense of the word. This means to say a genuinely Catholic attitude in matters of race

is one which concretely accepts and fully recognizes the fact that different races and cultures are *correlative. They mutually complete one another.* The white man needs the Negro, and needs to know that he needs him. White calls for black just as black calls for white. Our significance as white men is to be seen *entirely* in the fact that all men are not white. Until this fact is grasped, we will never realize our true place in the world, and we will never achieve what we are meant to achieve in it.[27]

With extraordinary sensitivity and sympathy, Merton listened to the voices of black Americans and tried with honesty to convey to a white American audience what they were saying during a time of social crisis. Seeking to communicate across a racial divide that many whites did not even perceive, he pressed on toward the ultimate end of communication: compassion and community, based on his own contemplative experience of the hidden wholeness of us all.

Like King, Merton attacked all three of the giant triplets: racism, extreme materialism, and militarism. His public entry into the antiwar movement was announced in a forceful essay, "The Root of War Is Fear," published in the October 1961 issue of the *Catholic Worker* and reprinted in the January 1, 1962 issue of *Fellowship*, the FOR's journal. Addressing the tensions brought on by the Cold War policy of nuclear deterrence, he lambasts the insanity of making peace by planning total war:

There is in reality not the slightest logical reason for war, and yet the whole world is plunging headlong into frightful destruction, and doing so *with the purpose of avoiding war and preserving peace!* This is a true war-madness, an illness of the mind and the spirit that is spreading with a furious and subtle contagion all over the world. . . . It does not even seem to enter our minds that there might be some incongruity in praying to the God of peace, the God who told us to love one another as He has loved us, who warned us that they who took the sword would perish by it, and at the same time planning to annihilate not thousands but millions . . . with the almost infallible certainty of inviting the same annihilation for ourselves. . . . So instead of loving what you think is peace, love other men and love God above all. And instead of hating the people you think are warmongers, hate the appetites and the disorder in your own soul, which are the causes of war. If you love peace, then hate injustice, hate tyranny, hate greed—but hate these things in *yourself*, not in another.[28]

Reminding us that we had been there before, Merton wrote a poem, "Original Child Bomb," on the atomic destruction of Hiroshima and Nagasaki, and another poem, "Chant to Be Used in Processions around a Site with Furnaces," making extensive use of the words of the commander at Auschwitz.

Like King, he spoke out vehemently against the US incursion in Vietnam, especially the indiscriminate burning of villages and use of napalm against civilians, which led him to conclude in an article published in the March 1968 issue of the *Catholic Worker* that the war was, as the title highlighted, "An Overwhelming Atrocity." A mentor of Jim Forest, he joined the Catholic Peace Fellowship that Forest helped form under the auspices of Muste and the FOR.

King's assassination in April 1968 prevented King and Merton from meeting. Merton died later that same year, electrocuted by a faulty fan while attending a monastic conference in Bangkok. Ironically, his body was flown home in a military jet, carrying the bodies of American soldiers killed in Vietnam. We will never know what joint word might have emerged from their encounter. But the complementarity of their visions, which is the subject of the next chapter, demonstrates that they were truly "soul brothers," who modeled the virtue of *compassion*. Merton was not just an astute analyst of the black liberation struggle; he profoundly empathized with that struggle as embodying the hidden wholeness of all persons and embraced the radical implications of compassion. Like King, he believed that beyond barriers of race, nationality, and religion, we must identify ourselves with the poor, the oppressed, and the wretched of the earth. It is our calling to become the voice of the voiceless, the face of the faceless, to an unheeding and uncaring society. Ultimately, according to Merton and King, "there are no aliens, no enemies, no others, but only sisters and brothers," as King claimed in his "Beyond Vietnam" speech at Riverside Church in New York City one year before his death. Both knew that this kind of identification, to be authentic as opposed to merely sentimental, requires action and self-sacrifice. Love in reality, unlike love in dreams, is a harsh and dreadful thing (as Elder Zosima and Day maintained). Compassion requires kenosis, self-emptying. Kenosis might take the shape of solitude and silence, as it did for Merton—the lonely self-emptying experience of nothingness that opens out into frightening darkness, which is light and emptiness, which is fullness. Or kenosis might take the form of altruistic activism, as it did for King—the daily burden of exhausting dedication to the schedules, needs, and demands of a cause that he knew would lead one day to his death. In either case, the self-emptying must take place. As both believed, the pattern had been set long ago by the person they tried to emulate, who "though he was in the form of God, did not count equality with God a thing to be grasped, but emptied himself, by taking the form of a servant, being born in the likeness of men. And being found in human form he humbled himself by becoming obedient to the point of death, even death on a cross" (Philippians 2:6–8).

Figure 6.1 Martin Luther King Jr. Peter Newark American Pictures / Bridgeman Images.

＊ CHAPTER 6 ＊

MARTIN LUTHER KING JR. AND THE CIVIL RIGHTS MOVEMENT
RELIGION IN US POLITICS

"And we shall overcome."
— President Lyndon Baines Johnson

I BEGIN THIS CHAPTER WITH THESE WORDS from "the anthem" of the US civil rights movement as emphatically intoned in a nationally televised speech before a joint session of the US Congress and a nationwide television audience in 1965 announcing a Voting Rights Bill. These words signaled the arrival of a victorious moment to all those who participated in the struggle, especially the countless, unsung, "ordinary" citizens who exhibited exemplary courage, dignity, and grace as they faced threats of violence and even death to gain their human and political rights. I emphasize their struggle lest my discussion of Martin Luther King Jr. reinforce the unfortunate tendency to excuse political inertia by the absence of a similar "charismatic" leader today. We must remember that King, as he frequently noted, did not make the movement, rather the movement made King. The major campaigns in Montgomery, Albany, Birmingham, Selma, Chicago, and Memphis were preceded by years of grassroots organization based on the development of local leadership, institutions, and protest networks before the arrival of King and his Southern Christian Leadership Conference (SCLC) staff.[1] Keeping this caveat in mind, it must be acknowledged that King formulated the most eloquent and enduring statement of the religious and political justification for nonviolent direct action to arise from the civil rights movement. He drew on both his biblical background formed in the African American church and his education in the philosophical and theological traditions acquired at Morehouse College, Crozer Theological Seminary, and Boston University. A major factor in the effectiveness of King's rhetoric was his remarkable fluency in both languages, his ability to cite Amos and Paul in one breath, and Plato and Henry David Thoreau in the next. Basing the civil rights struggle on the principles embedded in the biblical narratives of salvation history and the founding documents of the American republic, King demonstrated the moral force of a movement that many Americans saw as merely a political battle between two groups of extremists. He convincingly propounded the efficacy of the sacrifice ("the redemptive power of unmerited suffering") endured by the "martyrs of the movement" for the soul of the nation.

In a prescient essay published in 1943, A. J. Muste predicted that only the nonviolent suffering and bloodshed of African Americans along with their supporters would break the stronghold of Jim Crow in the United States:

> Thus it is that whenever love that will suffer unto death is manifested, whenever a true Crucifixion takes place, unconquerable power is released into the stream of history. The intuition that says that God has been let loose on the earth when such devotion is manifest is absolutely sound. This is the true road to liberation. Chiefly: mankind must always

depend on its minorities, on the downtrodden, to show the way, since the privileged are too much bound by their vested interests. . . . If the Negro churches of this country were to give the lead to their own people and their friends in the use of this basically Christian way of redemption, it would constitute another great step toward the achievement of a revolution greater and more beneficent than all the revolutions of the past.[2]

Twenty years later, Muste's prediction would be tested in the Deep South. On a Sunday morning, September 15, 1963, the congregation of 16th Street Baptist Church in Birmingham, Alabama, was busy preparing for Youth Day, an annual opportunity to honor the children of the congregation by giving them roles in conducting the service. The 16th Street Baptist Church had served as the rallying point for the civil rights demonstrations that had drawn national and indeed international attention, thanks to the cattle prods, clubs, fire hoses, and police dogs used by the police on demonstrators, many of them children, in the preceding months. It was a hopeful time for the movement. The March on Washington, one month earlier, had mobilized thousands of black and white supporters in front of the Lincoln Memorial in Washington, DC, signaling a national upsurge of support for desegregation. In Birmingham, protest leaders and city officials had finally signed a desegregation agreement one week earlier. After Sunday school, five girls stood checking their appearances in front of a mirror in the ladies room in the church basement. One girl was fixing the sash on another's dress. At 10:22 a.m., a tremendous blast shook the entire church. The bomb was so powerful that the outside brick-and-stone wall collapsed into the basement. Out of the rubble staggered twelve-year old Sarah Collins, calling the name of her sister, Addie Mae. Partially blinded and riddled with twenty-one pieces of broken glass, she was the only one in the room to survive. Four others died: Addie Mae Collins, fourteen; Carole Robertson, fourteen; Cynthia Wesley, fourteen; and Denise McNair, eleven. As news of the bombing spread across the nation and around the world, people of all races were moved to outrage by the tragedy. King remembered his immediate response:

> I shall never forget the grief and bitterness I felt on that terrible September morning. I think of how a woman cried out crunching through broken glass, "My God, we're not even safe in church!" I think of how that explosion blew the face of Jesus Christ from a stained glass window. I can remember thinking, was it all worth it? Was there any hope? . . . Where was God in the midst of bombs? . . . Our tradition, our faith, our loyalty were taxed that day as we gazed upon the caskets which held the bodies of those children. Some of us could not understand why God permitted death and destruction to come to those who had done no man harm.[3]

One week later, King attempted to articulate meaning in the deaths of the four young people as he delivered their funeral oration to a mourning congregation of blacks and whites as well as a national television audience:

> These children—unoffending, innocent and beautiful . . . are the martyred heroines of a holy crusade for freedom and human dignity. So they have something to say to us in their death. . . . They have something to say to every minister of the gospel who has remained silent behind the safe security of stained-glass windows. . . . They have something to say to each of us, black and white alike, that we must substitute

courage for caution . . . So they did not die in vain . . . History has proven over and over again that unmerited suffering is redemptive . . . We must not lose faith in our white brothers. Somehow we must believe that the most misguided among them can learn to respect the dignity and worth of all human personality.[4]

Coincidentally, the Sunday school lesson at 16th Street Baptist Church the day of the bombing was "The Love That Forgives."

On June 6, 1965, a new stained glass window was unveiled in the 16th Street Baptist Church. In the worldwide outpouring of grief and sympathy that followed the deaths of Collins, Robertson, Wesley, and McNair, the people of Wales donated a new window to replace the one of Christ shattered by the bomb blast. In the new window, the crucified figure of a black Christ was depicted, his left hand raised in protest, and his right hand extended in reconciliation. The inscription beneath the figure read "You Do It to Me," alluding in light and color to the words of Christ: "What you do to the least of these, you do to me."

(Justice came more slowly. Four Klansmen were identified as the main suspects in the bombing. Eventually three were brought to trial: one, Herman Frank, died in 1994; Robert Chambliss, who placed the bomb, was convicted of murder in 1977 by an Alabama court and died a decade later in jail; Thomas Blanton Jr. was found guilty in 2001; and Bobby Frank Cherry, at the age of seventy-one, was convicted of murder by a jury of nine whites and three blacks in 2002.)

The notions of citizen sacrifice and nonviolent protest were intertwined for both Muste and King, as methods of moving the conscience of the oppressors and the guilty bystanders to empathize with the oppressed and act to change the entrenched legal structure of white supremacy. The notion of sacrifice for the nation is of course a well-established description of military service. The civil rights movement exemplified the sacrifice of civilians for the basic principle of democracy: justice and freedom for all. No less than those willing to die for these values on foreign shores, here were citizens, including children, willing to die for them at home.

As King (echoing Thoreau and Mahatma Gandhi) outlined it, nonviolence required active resistance to evil instead of passivity; it sought to convert, not to defeat, the opponent; it was directed against evil, not against persons; and it avoided internal violence, such as hatred or bitterness, as much as external violence, because hatred depersonalized the individual. Nonviolence, according to King, was based on the belief that acceptance of suffering was redemptive, because suffering could transform both the sufferer and the oppressor; it was based on loving others regardless of worth or merit; it was premised on the realization that all human beings are interrelated; and it was grounded in the confidence that justice would, in the end, triumph over injustice. The hopeful refrain "The arc of the universe bends slowly but it bends toward justice" that he repeated so often, became a mantra. The belief that suffering was redemptive was crucial to King as the rational for nonviolent direct action. By accepting the violence of the oppressor, without retaliation and even without hatred, the demonstrators, he insisted, could transform the oppressor's heart.[5]

The deaths in Birmingham were not the first nor would they be the last to mark the civil rights era. The reaction of the public to the unmerited suffering of black citizens as dramatized in the public arena by civil rights protesters is one indication of the effectiveness of black protest in changing the minds and hearts of some Americans. Perhaps the greatest demonstration of national action in reaction to racist-inspired violence against peaceful protesters for civil rights occurred two years after Birmingham.

In January 1965, African American residents of Selma and the surrounding black belt counties took the first steps in a campaign to gain the right to vote—a right denied them by a system of apartheid that prevailed in Alabama for as long as they could remember. Mobilized by civil rights workers from the SCLC and the Student Nonviolent Coordinating Committee, increasing numbers of local black people risked their jobs, homes, physical safety, and very lives for merely registering to vote. Rejected time and again by white registrars, they joined together in marches and peaceful demonstrations to protest their disenfranchisement—a persistent reminder of the intransigent rule of white supremacy.[6]

On February 17, Alabama state troopers, wielding billy clubs, attacked a group of marchers in nearby Marion. "Negroes could be heard screaming and loud whacks rang through the square," reported a newspaper correspondent from the scene. When twenty-six-year-old Jimmie Lee Jackson rushed to protect his mother, Viola, and his eighty-two-year-old grandfather, Cager Lee, from being beaten, a trooper shot him twice in the stomach. He was taken to the Good Samaritan Hospital in Selma, where he died on February 26. In response to Jackson's death, SCLC leaders conceived a plan to march from Selma to the state capitol of Montgomery, a distance of fifty-four miles. On Sunday, March 7, a group of marchers started across the Edmund Pettus Bridge toward Route 80, the highway to Montgomery. They were met on the bridge by a large contingent of

Alabama state troopers and local police. After warning the marchers to disperse, the police charged the crowd, releasing tear gas and beating people senseless with clubs. Televised on the evening news, images of "Bloody Sunday," as the event came to be known, stirred widespread shame and anger. King issued a nationwide call for religious and civic leaders to come to Selma to participate in another march, scheduled for Tuesday, March 9.

Among the hundreds of clergy responding to King's invitation was Reverend James Reeb, a thirty-eight-year-old Unitarian minister who worked as a community organizer for the Friends Service Committee in the inner-city neighborhoods of Boston. Reeb not only worked to improve housing in poor black neighborhoods; he insisted on living there as well, with his wife and their four small children. The second march was brief. Due to a temporary restraining order prohibiting a Selma to Montgomery march, King and his advisers decided to march only to the point of confrontation with the police. Facing the state troopers and police force once again on the Edmund Pettus Bridge, the marchers turned and retreated to a mass meeting at Brown Chapel AME Church. There King asked those who had come from afar to remain until a final decision on the legality of the march to Montgomery came down from the court.

That night, three white men attacked Reeb and two other Unitarian ministers outside a Ku Klux Klan hangout in Selma. Clubbed to the ground, Reeb suffered a massive concussion. His death two days later prompted a national uproar. President Lyndon Baines Johnson went on national television to decry Reeb's murder. That evening, Johnson spoke before a nationally televised joint session of Congress, delivering perhaps the most powerful address ever given by a US president against segregation. After lamenting the death of Reeb as an "American tragedy," Johnson acknowledged that

> the real hero of the struggle is the American Negro. His action and protests, his courage to risk safety and even to risk his life, have awakened the conscience of the Nation. His demonstrations have been designed to call attention to injustice, designed to provoke change, designed to stir reform. He has called upon us to make good the promise of America. And who among us can say that we would have made the same progress were it not for his persistent bravery and his faith in American democracy.[7]

Johnson announced that he would immediately submit a voting rights bill to Congress and urged in the strongest terms that it be passed. He acknowledged that he fully anticipated opposition, but predicted deliberately and forcefully after pausing to look directly into the television camera, "And we *shall* overcome." Watching the speech on television in a Selma motel room, King and his closest lieutenants wept.

On Monday, March 15, a memorial service for Reeb was held in Brown Chapel AME Church. Once again King delivered the main eulogy, although distinguished leaders, who had gathered from around the country, also spoke of the meaning of Reeb's death, and linked arms to sing "We Shall Overcome" and other movement hymns.

Local black citizens deeply appreciated the presence of white demonstrators in Selma, even though they were keenly aware of the disparity between the national outpouring of publicity and grief over the death of Reeb, a white man, compared to the sparse attention devoted to the death of Jackson, a black man. Several days after the memorial service, a federal court order was issued permitting the march to Montgomery, and the nation watched as white and black Americans joined in the "high-water mark" of nonviolent southern protest in the civil rights movement as people spent five days walking to Montgomery, eventually reaching a crowd of twenty-five thousand gathered at the statehouse, the symbolic capitol of the old Confederacy.

That movement, described by King, Thomas Merton, and Abraham Joshua Heschel as a kairos moment—a time of special divine providence—has served, along with the nineteenth-century abolitionist movement, as a paradigm of religious activism for social justice in the public square. Although many saw it as merely political, King and those who embraced his vision interpreted the movement as a moral struggle, a "God-given cause" that moved citizens of different ethnic, racial, and religious distinctions to act together to form local grassroots organizations as well as larger national networks in a massive effort to achieve justice for those fellow citizens long denied equal access to "life, liberty, and the pursuit of happiness."

Current distrust of the role of religion in politics is focused on the divisive force of hot-button issues, such as abortion, gay and lesbian rights, school prayer, "family values," the putative "secularization" of American society, and the role of the religious right in electoral politics, augmented by the intemperate and emotional, if not vitriolic, language of print, radio, television, and Internet commentators, who increase and arouse their audiences by frequently belittling, ridiculing, and demonizing those with whom they disagree. In this atmosphere, comity, trust, civility, and fellow regard, necessary habits for democratic discourse, cannot thrive. In both historical paradigms of the role of religion in politics that I've mentioned, the mid-nineteenth-century antislavery movement and mid-twentieth-century civil rights movement, whites were enabled to empathize vicariously with the suffering of African Americans.

To my mind, one of the most empathic interpreters of King and the civil rights movement generally was someone from a quite-different background than King's or those he led. Merton, cloistered in a Cistercian monastery in Kentucky, perceived with exceptional insight the historical challenge of the civil rights movement, and in a series of rhetorically powerful essays, enunciated a vision of the state of American democracy that converged with that of King. Our current situation desperately needs the coherence of their visions, which models a kind of communication across differences of racial, vocational, and biographical backgrounds.

King was born in Atlanta, Georgia, in 1929, the son of Alberta Williams King and Martin Luther King Sr., pastor of Ebenezer Baptist Church.[8] Compared to Merton's, King's childhood was happy and secure, though all too early he was made aware of the hurts inflicted by racism. Like his father, grandfather, and great-grandfather, King entered the ministry, and throughout the years of his leadership in the civil rights movement, he remained a preacher, regularly occupying the pulpit for Sunday worship, and drawing on the black church tradition in which he was formed for both the style and content of the political speeches he delivered at demonstrations and appearances in the public square. Courses in philosophy, ethics, and theology at Morehouse College, Crozer Theological Seminary, and Boston University provided King with the opportunity to develop an intellectual framework for the systematic analysis of the relationship between Christianity and society, but the existential base for his commitment to social justice was already established in the tradition of black religious protest exemplified by his father's and grandfather's embrace of Social Gospel activism. Strongly attracted to the intellectual life, King might have combined ministerial and academic careers by choosing job offers at schools in the North, but in 1954, he chose instead to accept the fateful call to pastor Dexter Avenue Baptist Church in Montgomery.

The Abbey of Our Lady of Gethsemani and Dexter Avenue Baptist Church represent two different locations and traditions that nonetheless held a significant trait in common: their marginality. Monks were marginal by profession; they had rejected the dominant values of the world—money, status, power, fame, and luxury. African Americans were marginalized by discrimination in a society shot through with the ideology and habits of white supremacy. Both were profoundly extraneous to the priorities and values of mainstream America in the 1950s. Marginality provided both men with the critical distance necessary for radical dissent from the religious and political status quo. Moreover, the contemplative tradition of monasticism and protest tradition within African American religion furnished Merton and King, respectively, the spiritual insight necessary to articulate convincing critical analyses of society, and the religious experience necessary to ground their prescriptions for social change in personal commitment.

Yet it was not the traditions per se but rather what Merton and King took from them, or better, the ways in which they were transformed, that made all the difference. Initially, neither Merton nor King set out to "save the soul of the nation." There was in the young Merton the enthusiasm of the convert, which led him to espouse in his earlier works, including his best-selling autobiography, *The Seven Storey Mountain* (1948), a world-rejecting attitude that he later came to recant, realizing that "no man can withdraw completely from the society of his fellow men; and the monastic community is deeply implicated, for better or for worse, in the economic, political, and social structures of the contemporary world." Merton had learned (as epitomized in the Fourth and Walnut "revelation" mentioned in the previous chapter) that it was the particular task of the contemplative monk, as a man on the margins, to speak out of his silence and solitude with an independent voice in order to clarify for those who were "completely immersed in other cares" the true value of the human person amid the illusions with which mass society surrounds modern people at every turn.[9]

King's life, like Merton's, was turned from its expected trajectory—in his case, by an unexpected event: the 1955 Montgomery bus boycott, which King neither started nor suggested, but that irrevocably changed him from the successful pastor of a moderately comfortable congregation to the leader of a national movement for racial justice. As spokesman for the boycott, King was overwhelmed by threats against his life and his family. Reaching the end of his endurance, he sat at his kitchen table late one night over a cup of coffee, trying to figure out how to escape his role without appearing a coward.

> And I discovered then that religion had to become real to me, and I had to know God for myself. And I bowed over that cup of coffee. I never will forget it. . . . I prayed, . . . "Lord, I'm down here trying to do what's right. I think the cause that we represent is right. But Lord, I must confess that I'm weak now. I'm faltering. I'm losing my courage. And I can't let the people see me like this because if they see me weak and losing my courage they will begin to get weak." And it seemed at that moment that I could hear an inner voice saying to me, "Martin Luther, stand up for righteousness.

Stand up for justice. Stand up for truth. And lo, I will be with you, even until the end of the world." . . . I heard the voice of Jesus saying still to fight on. He promised never to leave me, never to leave me alone. No never alone. No never alone. He promised never to leave me, never to leave me alone. Almost at once my fears began to go. My uncertainty disappeared.[10]

Both men underwent experiences that widened and deepened their understanding of the paths they had begun. King committed himself to the movement completely despite his growing realization—more certain as the years went by—that it would cost him his life. Convinced that the monk left the world for the sake of the world, Merton devoted himself and his writing, despite public criticism and censorship from his superiors, to trenchant critique of political issues. Both paths converged initially on the issue of civil rights. Merton as well as King perceived civil rights as a moral and religious struggle, indeed as *the* religious cause of the day—a view disputed by many Christians, who saw it as an essentially secular issue, off-limits for a cloistered monk. On the contrary, Merton shared with King a profound belief that in the civil rights movement, the nation was living through a time of providential testing and opportunity: "In the Negro Christian non-violent movement, under Martin Luther King, [Merton proclaimed] the *kairos*, the 'providential time,' met with a courageous and enlightened response. The non-violent Negro civil rights drive has been one of the most positive and successful expressions of Christian faith in action in the social history of the United States."[11]

According to King, the struggle for civil rights presented the nation with an unprecedented historical opportunity: "The problem of race and color prejudice remains America's greatest moral dilemma. When one considers the impact it has on our nation, internally and externally, its resolution might well determine our destiny History has thrust upon our generation an indescribably important task—to complete a process of democratization which our nation has too long developed too slowly."[12] But, both men warned, the moment could be lost, and if it were, the consequences would be dire. The moment, according to Merton, will pass without effect, and "the merciful kairos of truth will turn into the dark hour of destruction and hate."[13]

The concept of kairos gave a sense of urgency ("the urgency of now") to their calls for a national renewal that could only come about through nonviolent direct action. Merton shared King's admiration for Gandhi and his philosophy and life of nonviolence. Nonviolence for both was the only method that respected the dignity, and indeed the sacredness, of the person. In concert, they lambasted current attitudes and behaviors that debased human freedom and deadened human consciousness, especially the mindless striving after power, status, and wealth—and consumerism, which they described as a dangerous collective illusion that effectively reduces persons to objects, and relegates interpersonal relationships to manipulation and exploitation. In short, King warned, "We need to move from a thing-oriented society to a person-oriented society."[14] In his essay "Rain and the Rhinoceros," inspired by the sound of the rain in the woods surrounding his hermitage and mindful of Thoreau's cabin on Walden Pond, Merton diagnosed consumerism as a futile attempt to forget our condition of radical contingency, to suppress our awareness of the inevitability of our death. Consumerism works by "creating an illusion of yourself as one who has no needs that you cannot immediately fulfill. Artificial needs are created, typically by mass media, and then 'satisfied,' thus holding out the spurious promise of omnipotence, but actually drawing the consumer into a spiraling cycle of need-gratification-need that can only lead to frustration and end in despair. Trapped in this vicious cycle, we are burdened by illusion and conditioned to 'suffer all the needs that society demands we suffer.' "[15]

For Merton, as for King, commitment to nonviolence affirmed the preciousness of each human life—an intuition rising out of his own contemplative experience of the presence of God at the still point (*le pointe vierge*) of each person. King based his belief in the value of the human person on our common identity as children of God, made in God's image and so worthy of respect. "Every man is somebody, because he is a child of God."[16] The image of God "is universally shared in equal portions by all. . . . Every human being has etched in his personality the indelible stamp of the Creator." If any person is "treated as anything less than a person of sacred worth, the image of God is abused in him and consequently and proportionally lost by those who inflict this abuse."[17]

Human relationships, then, should be ruled by love—love defined not as affection but rather as "an understanding, redeeming good will for all. . . . It is an entirely 'neighbor-regarding concern for others,' which discovers the neighbor in every man it meets. . . . When I speak of love," King explained, "I am not speaking of some sentimental and weak response. I am speaking of that force which all of the great religions have seen as the unifying principle of life. Love is somehow the key that unlocks the door which leads to ultimate reality. This Hindu-Muslim-Christian-Jewish-Buddhist belief about ultimate reality is beautifully summed up in the first epistle of Saint John: 'Let us love one another for love is of God and everything that loves is born of God and knows God.'"[18] Thus not only acts of violence but also internal attitudes, such as hate or bitterness, and even resentment, had to be abandoned because they contradicted the internal logic of personality and the ordering law of the universe. (How different than the physical violence of the white supremacist then or the verbal violence of the political ideologue today.)

For both Merton and King, the interrelatedness of human beings—the hidden wholeness that binds us all together—is key to understanding and accepting our responsibility for social justice. In King's words, "Whether we call it an unconscious process, an impersonal Brahman, or a Personal Being of matchless power and infinite love, there is a creative force in this universe that works to bring the disconnected aspects of reality into a harmonious whole." He went on to assert, "All life is interrelated. All men are caught in an inescapable network of mutuality, tied in a single garment of destiny."[19]

Belief in our fundamental interrelatedness moved King and Merton to take a universalist perspective on the social problems of their (and our) era. They perceived clearly the connection between the struggle for civil rights in the United States and the independence struggles of colonized peoples around the world. Earlier than most, they pointed out the link between violence at home and violence abroad, as they insisted on speaking out against what Merton called an overwhelming atrocity, the Vietnam War. Recognition of the interrelatedness of all persons, they claimed, lays on all people of goodwill the radical obligation of compassion.

At the time of King's assassination, mutual Quaker friends were arranging a visit and short rest/retreat for King with Merton and the Vietnamese Buddhist monk Thich Nhat

Hanh at the monastery of Gethsemani. The news of King's death devastated Merton. He immediately sent a note of condolence to Coretta Scott King. "Let me only say how deeply I share your personal grief as well as the shock, which pervades the whole nation. He has done the greatest thing anyone can do. In imitation of his master he has laid down his life for friends and enemies. . . . He will go down in history as one of our greatest citizens."[20] Note Merton's encomium of King as both an exemplary Christian and citizen.

The struggle to overcome "the giant triplets of racism, excess materialism, and militarism" remains arduous. It requires the radical realization that alienation from our true selves, fed and disguised by mass consumerism, leads to violence and the reduction of persons into things. Contemplation and action need to be joined lest our activism becomes merely another form of violence and our contemplation another form of self-gratification. Contemplative silence, solitude and simplicity (as Thoreau long ago argued) are necessary in order to come into contact with the true self. But action is also required in identification with, solidarity with, and presence among the poor, the oppressed, and the victims of injustice, lest we remain guilty bystanders, obsessed by our desire to satisfy "spiritual" hedonism, no less than material hedonism.

Kairos time may be accurate if it leads to urgency, but misleading if we use it as an excuse for inaction. "The time has passed; the movement is over." It is not over, unless it is over in our lives. The struggle goes on in local communities across the nation, just as it did before the movement began. Hopeful examples exist in the activism of the Industrial Areas Foundation chapters and similar networks of organizing for social change that continue to crop up across the nation. Typically based in existing congregations, churches, synagogues, mosques, and temples, the foundation is non-partisan but resolutely political in encouraging local people to meet to identify issues of concern. Citizens are encouraged to speak of their own experiences, tell their own stories to encourage empathy, and raise the possibility of imagining change in their lives. Additional home meetings serve to identify and recruit leaders from the community, based on the principle "never do for others what they can do for themselves." Mass meetings are structured to hold public officials accountable for problems of concern. The Industrial Areas Foundation has fifty-nine affiliates active across the United States, Canada, the United Kingdom, Australia, and Germany. My colleague at Princeton, Jeffrey Stout, told the foundation's story in his book, *Blessed Are the Organized*. Also on the international level another organization comes to mind, the Community of Sant'Egidio, which began as a prayer for peace group in Rome in 1968, and now has branches active around the world in serving the poor and brokering peace agreements among battling opponents, as it did in Mozambique several years back.

The sacrifices of those exemplars in the civil rights struggle must not lie immured in amber in civil rights museums, but recalled to life in the many sacrificial acts, small and large, by which we seek to "re-member" our sundered communities, and in James Baldwin's memorable phrase, "achieve our country and change the history of the world."[21]

The civil rights movement exemplifies for us the faculty of empathy, nourished through the telling of and listening to each other's stories. Learning and practicing the habits and virtues of citizenship and democratic process must happen from childhood on. If we hold leaders and each other accountable to their promises and obligations; if we treat opponents not as enemies but rather as potential allies; if we trust to civil discussion and do not shy away from argument based on different opinions, values, and religious beliefs that are as important to others as our own are to us; if each listens carefully to each, with respect and forbearance; if we encourage one another in speaking truth to power, no matter the danger; and if we keep faith that change is possible, when we work for it no matter how long and hard the odds seem— then we too, like those exemplars remembered in these pages, "shall overcome."

Figure 7.1 Fannie Lou Hamer. Ken Thompson / General Board of Global Ministries of the United Methodist Church.

CHAPTER 7

"IS THIS AMERICA?"

FANNIE LOU HAMER AND THE VOICES OF LOCAL PEOPLE

The Spirit of the Lord is upon me, because he has anointed me to proclaim good news to the poor. He has sent me to proclaim liberty to the captives and recovering of sight to the blind, to set at liberty those who are oppressed.

—Luke 4:28

COTTON FIELDS STRETCH AS FAR AS THE EYE CAN SEE. Waves of heat beat down on the bent backs of black sharecroppers, steadily plucking the white bolls in the breezeless humid air. Battered straw hats and head rags offer scant protection from the unrelenting Mississippi Delta sun. For generations they have labored from daybreak to first dark, eking out a bare subsistence working the white man's land, and living in dilapidated wood shacks without running water or indoor toilets. Mississippi, where brutal violence customarily suppressed any and all challenges to white supremacy, and where law or subterfuge blocked any attempts by black people to vote; Mississippi, whose rivers, the Tallahatchie, Big Black, Yazoo, and Mississippi, held untold numbers of mutilated black bodies. On October 6, 1917, Fannie Lou Townsend, the youngest child of a sharecropping family, was born in Tommolen,

Montgomery County, Mississippi. All told, her parents, James Lee Townsend and Lou Ella (Bramlett) Townsend, had twenty children (six girls and fourteen boys). When she was two years old, the family moved to Ruleville in Sunflower County, where she would spend the rest of her life. In addition to sharecropping, her father served as a Baptist preacher and sold bootleg whiskey on the side to help make ends meet. Still, there was little money to support the large family. Hamer recalled how her mother coped with their constant hunger: "So many times for dinner we would have greens with no seasonin' . . . and flour gravy. My mother would mix flour with a little grease and try to make gravy out of it. Sometimes she'd cook a little meal and we'd have bread."[1]

Hamer joined her parents and siblings in the fields at the age of six, after the landowner offered her a reward of Cracker Jacks, gingerbread, and candy if she could pick 30 pounds of cotton in a week. "I picked that. . . . Then the next week I was asked to pick 60 lbs. and by the time I was 13 years old, I was picking 200–300 lbs. of cotton a day." The seasonal demands of crop picking restricted black children's attendance at school to four months a year: December, January, February, and March. And "for most of that time," she recalled, "we never had shoes." [2] They wrapped their feet in rags, and wore tattered clothes patched with patches on top of patches. In the segregated public school system of Mississippi, black students received less than 20 percent of the funding allotted for white students, who attended three months longer than black children. Nonetheless, Hamer enjoyed school, especially spelling and reading. Due to financial pressure, she left her one-room schoolhouse after six years, at the age of twelve. That same year, she was baptized in the Quiver River and her only further formal education occurred in Bible study classes at the Strangers' Home Baptist Church, the source of her familiarity with the biblical texts and hymns she deployed, by chapter and verse, so naturally and frequently in interviews and speeches for years to come.

The example of Hamer's parents, especially her mother, reinforced her self-esteem weakened by the pervasive white supremacy of the environment:

> I really didn't know what everything was about but I just couldn't understand why Black people worked so hard and never had nothing. I just couldn't understand why the white people that weren't working were always riding in nice cars, two or three cars, and a truck. I just couldn't understand. They had everything, and it seemed that we worked all the time and didn't have nothing. There must have been something wrong with us. Then one day I asked my mother how come we weren't white. She told me that there was nothing in the world wrong with being Black. And she said, "You might not understand what I'm talking about now, but you will one day. I want you to respect yourself as a Black child, and as you get older, you respect yourself as a Black woman. If you respect yourself enough, other people will have to respect you."[3]

She added: "Be grateful that you are black. If God had wanted you to be white, you would have been white, so you accept yourself for what you are." Her mother reinforced her message by singing: "I would not be a white man / I'll tell you the reason why / I'm afraid my lord might would call me / and I wouldn't be ready to die. They ain't got God in their heart / To hell they sure must go."[4] Years later Hamer recalled tenderly that her mother had given her a black doll, the first she'd ever seen.

As a child, aware of the constant threat of violence, Hamer was amazed and reassured by her mother's total commitment to protecting her children. Although people thought her mother was crazy for standing up to the white man, she was fiercely determined to protect her children from mistreatment. Her mother went to the field every morning balancing a pan on her head and carrying two buckets in her hands. One of the buckets was always covered. One day, Hamer, curious, peeked inside and was shocked to discover a 9mm Luger that her mother took with her to the field every day. It was her first lesson in self-defense. She knew her mother was deeply religious, but she would not allow anyone to harm her children. Years later, Hamer recalled a telling example of her mother's amazing courage:

> One day this man had come out to the field, he was on a horse . . . and he told my mother he was coming out there to get one of her nieces. "You know I come out here to get Pauline today and I'm going to make her go back home but I'm goin' to give her a good whipping first." My mother just stood there . . . and said, "You don't have no Black children and you not goin' to beat no Black children. If you step down off of that horse I'll go to Hell and back with you, before Hell can scorch a feather." And he didn't get down. But she would have done just what she said. This was the kind of way she felt and I really feel that just had a lot to do with me being what I am today, whatever that is.[5]

She also recalled another experience that revealed to her the stranglehold white supremacy held on the chances of black sharecroppers to get ahead. Her family experienced a brief period of upward mobility during her early teen years, only to see it blocked by a white neighbor's malice. Her parents finally were able to save enough money to buy three mules, a wagon, and a cultivator. Her father hoped they would have a chance to buy a house. They moved out of the plantation cabin they were staying in to move into another one while theirs was being repaired. All their livestock stayed behind, and a white neighbor poured an insecticide into the feed, killing their cow and three mules. They never were able to get back on their feet again. "That white man did it just because we were gettin' somewhere. White people never like to see Negroes get a little success. All of this stuff is no secret in the state of Mississippi."[6]

In 1944, at the age of twenty-seven, Fannie Lou Townsend married Perry (Pap) Hamer, a farmer and tractor driver, who was thirty-two. They settled on W. D. Marlow's plantation outside Ruleville, where she was hired as the timekeeper, keeping track of work hours, the amount of cotton picked by each field hand, and the amount of pay due each worker. In that position, she was able to surreptitiously gauge the accurate weight of the cotton the hands picked to circumvent the owner's habit of lowering the total weight of each bale. In addition, she worked as a domestic in the landlord's household and an insurance agent in the black community. She and Pap took in two children to care for as well as her mother, who died in 1951. During that same year, Hamer entered the hospital to have a cyst removed from her stomach. Without her knowledge or permission, the doctor performed a hysterectomy on her—a common practice in Mississippi at the time.

The arrival of civil rights activists in Sunflower County in 1961 initiated a momentous change in the life of Hamer and her community. On a Monday night, August 27, 1962, a mass meeting was held at Williams Chapel Missionary Baptist Church to discuss black voter registration in Sunflower County. Organizers at the meeting included James Bevel from the Southern Christian Leadership Conference (SCLC), Amzie Moore from the National Association for the Advancement of Colored People (NAACP), Dave Dennis from the Congress of Racial Equality (CORE), and Bob Moses, Reginald Robinson, and James Forman from the Student Nonviolent Coordinating Committee (SNCC). (The four groups formed an umbrella organization called the Council of Federated Organizations [COFO].) Bevel preached a sermon based on Luke 12:54–56: "He also said to the crowds, 'When you see a cloud rising in the west, you say at once, "A shower is coming," and so it happens. And when you see the south wind blowing, you say, "There will be scorching heat," and it happens. You hypocrites! You know how to interpret the appearance of earth and sky, but why do you not know how to interpret the present time?' " Hamer remembered that "it was a beautiful sermon." The sermon was effectively arguing, in concrete agricultural images the congregation well understood, that the time for change was now. After others spoke, Forman talked about the constitutional right of black citizens to register and vote. As Forman spoke about the Fifteenth Amendment to the US Constitution, which Hamer had never heard of, "I made up my mind that this was something important to me. And it seemed like it was something that I wanted to take a chance on."[7] Eighteen people decided that night to risk their jobs, homes, and possibly lives to become first-class citizens by registering to vote. Before leaving the church, the volunteers received instructions on how to fill out the voter registration form and then signed a list committing themselves to register on the following Friday.

On the morning of August 31, they boarded a bus to travel from Ruleville to the county courthouse in Indianola twenty-six miles away. The bus, owned by a black man, had been used for years, without incident, to carry cotton pickers to the fields in summer, and from Mississippi to Florida in winter when the land lay fallow and they couldn't earn enough money locally to feed their families. When they arrived in Indianola, all eighteen of the would-be registrants got off the bus and entered the courthouse, but the registrar announced that only two at a time could take the test. Hamer and Ernest Davis, a young volunteer, stayed to take "the literacy test" first. The test consisted of twenty-one questions. As Hamer explained: "It began 'What is your full name?' 'Write the date of the application.' Then it went on to questions such as: 'By whom are you employed?'—meaning you would be fired by the time you got back home. 'Where is your place of residence in this district?'—this meant that the Ku Klux Klan and White Citizen's Council would be given your address." After they answered that kind of question, the clerk pointed out a section of the Mississippi Constitution, and told them to copy it and then give a reasonable interpretation of it. For Hamer, it was the first time that she learned that Mississippi even had a constitution. It took the eighteen volunteers until 4:30 p.m. to finish the process. They boarded the bus and headed back home, but were stopped two miles out of Indianola by policemen, who ordered them all off the bus and then ordered them back on the bus to return to Indianola, where the bus driver was fined a hundred dollars for driving a bus that was the wrong color—too yellow and thus possible to be confused with a school bus. When no one had that much money, the fine was reduced to thirty dollars, which the eighteen chipped in to pay. Back home in Ruleville, Hamer was greeted by her adopted daughter Dorothy, who told her that the landowner, Marlow, was "blazing mad" because she had tried to register and because he feared reprisals by the Klan against himself. Later that evening he accosted her: "You'll have to go back down there and withdraw that thing, or you'll have to leave." Hamer recalled

> that was what really did it for me. I just thought to myself, "what does he really care about us?" I had been workin' there

for eighteen years. I had baked cakes and sent them overseas to him during the war. I had nursed his family, cleaned his house, stayed with his kids. I had handled his time book and his payroll. Yet he wanted me out. I made up my mind I was grown, and I was tired. I wouldn't go back. In a little while he came to the house, ravin' mad, tellin' me I'd have to withdraw, and I said to him, "I didn't go down there to register for you. I went down there to register for myself."[8]

Her response, as scholar Maegan Parker Brooks insightfully suggests, may have alluded to a familiar spiritual from childhood: "I'm going down to the river of Jordan / Yes, I'm going down there for myself. / Oh, I got to stand my test in the judgment / Oh, I got to stand it for myself. / There's nobody else that can go there for me / I've got to stand it for myself."[9] Marlow fired her on the spot. She left her home that very night. On September 10, the home of Mr. and Mrs. Robert Tucker, where she was staying, was riddled with sixteen bullets, and two black girls were shot the same night.[10] Given the imminent threat from night riders, Pap convinced her to leave Ruleville with their two daughters to stay with her niece in Sumner in Tallahatchie County. There SNCC fieldworker Charles McLaurin, who had accompanied the would-be registrants on the bus to Indianola and noted Hamer's ability to calm their fears by leading them in song, tracked her down and invited her to attend a civil rights conference at Fisk University in Nashville, organized by SNCC for local leaders from across the South. She accepted immediately, and in a few minutes had packed and was ready to leave. Surprised, McLaurin asked her later if she had known he was coming. Her reply that she knew God had sent him shocked him into responding that it was Moses who had sent him. "Well, God sent Bob Moses" was her immediate reply. Recognizing her gifts, SNCC volunteers, influenced by Ella Baker's model of local grassroots autonomy rather than top-down (often-clerical) hierarchy, encouraged her leadership. After speaking at several colleges about her experiences trying to register to vote, she returned to Ruleville.

Unsurprisingly, she had failed the first registration test, but undeterred she returned on December 4 and took it again, warning the registrar, "You'll see me every 30 days till I pass." When she returned on January 10, she learned that she had passed, but couldn't vote in the next election because she didn't have two consecutive poll tax receipts. Reprisals against her and her family included frequent drive-by threats from night riders, early morning raids by police officers with drawn guns, the arrest and jailing of Pap for a fraudulent overdue $2,000 water bill, and death threats in the mail. Unable to can food that the family desperately needed, with Pap unemployable because he was Hamer's husband, getting by during winter 1962 was hard. Not dissuaded by the continuous harassment of segregationists, she took on an increasingly active role in organizing grassroots support for registration in the Mississippi Delta as a field secretary at large for COFO and a teacher in SCLC-sponsored citizenship schools based on the model developed by educator Septima Clark.

In June 1963, she and seven other civil rights activists attended a five-day residential workshop on citizenship schools, led by Clark and her niece Bernice Robinson, cosponsored by the SCLC and the Highlander Research Center, and held at the Sea Island Center on Johns Island, near Charleston, South Carolina. She had attended a similar training session a few months earlier in Dorchester, Georgia, led by civil rights activists Clark, Dorothy Cotton, and Andrew and Jean Young. Returning home by bus on June 9, they were stopped, and six people, including Hamer, were arrested and jailed in Winona, Mississippi, the headquarters of the White Citizens' Council of the state, located in Montgomery County, sixty miles east of Indianola, the county in which she had been born. Hamer repeated the story of what happened next in interviews and public appearances around the country, and—as we will see—most significantly on nationwide television:

> I was placed in a cell. . . . And I began to hear some of the saddest and some of the loudest screams and sounds I'd ever heard in my life. And finally they passed my cell, with . . . June Johnson, fifteen years old. Her clothes was torn off of her waist, and the blood was running from her head down in her bosom, and they put her in a cell. And then I began to hear somebody else when they would scream and I would hear a voice say, "Can't you say 'yes, sir,' nigger?" And I understood [SCLC worker] Miss [Annelle] Ponder's voice, and she said, "Yes, I can say, 'yes, sir.'" "So why don't you say it?" And she said, "I don't know you well enough." And I don't know how long they beat Miss Ponder, but I would hear her body when it would hit the floor, and I would just hear the screams, and I will never forget something that Miss Ponder said during the time that they were beating her. She asked God to have mercy on those people because they didn't know what they was doing. And finally, they passed my cell, and . . . her clothes were ripped from the shoulder down, one of her eyes looked like blood and her mouth was swollen almost like my hand. . . . I was led out of that cell into another . . . where they had two black prisoners. The state highway patrolman ordered me to lay down on the bunk bed on my face, and he ordered the first prisoner to beat me. The black prisoner said, "Do you want me to beat this woman with this?" It was a long leather blackjack with some kind of metal, and . . . he

said, "If you don't beat her . . . you don't know what we will do to you." The first prisoner began to beat me, and he beat me until he was exhausted. I was steady trying to hold my hands behind my back to try to protect myself from some of the terrible blows that I was getting in my back. And after the first prisoner was exhausted, I thought that was all. . . . And the second prisoner began to beat . . . and I couldn't control the sobs then because I was screaming and couldn't stop. . . . And during the time the second one was beating . . . my dress worked up real high behind my body. And I had never been exposed to five mens in one room in my life, because one thing my parents taught me when I was a child was dignity and respect. And during the time my dress worked up and I smoothed my dress down, one of the white men . . . pulled my dress up, and . . . one of the white men was trying to feel under my clothes. They beat me, they beat me, and I couldn't hush. And then one of the men . . . walked over and began to beat me in the head. I remember wrapping my face down in a pillow . . . where I could muffle out the sounds. I don't know how long this lasted, but I remember . . . the same cop was standing there cussing, telling me to get up. At first it didn't seem like I could get up because at this point my hands was navy blue, and I couldn't even bend my fingers. And he kept telling me to "get up bitch. You can walk, get up, fatso!" . . . They carried me back to my cell . . . and just to bend my knees forward, you could hear me screaming I don't know how far."[11]

The other four passengers on the bus were not arrested and informed the local SCLC office of what had happened when they reached Greenwood. Lawrence Guyot, one of the first SNCC fieldworkers in the state, hurried to Winona to try to get them released. He was arrested instead and severely beaten like the rest. As he passed her cell, Hamer caught a glimpse of his bloodied face and remarked that this was one of the only times she had not seen him smiling. Hamer and the other badly injured prisoners were charged with disorderly conduct and resisting arrest, and held in jail without medical attention from Sunday to Wednesday. Hamer suffered permanent damage to her kidneys and a blood clot on a nerve in her left eye. During their imprisonment, they tried to strengthen their spirits by singing spirituals and freedom songs based by Hamer's strong voice. Identifying with the persecution of the first Christians, they took solace from verses like "Paul and Silas Bound in Jail / No one to go their bail / Keep your eyes on the prize; hold on." The wife of the sheriff surreptitiously brought them water and ice, and confessed to Hamer that she was trying to lead a good Christian life. Hamer responded by recommending that she write down two Bible passages and read them later: Proverbs 26:26, "Though his hatred be covered with deception, his wickedness will be exposed in the assembly," and one of her favorites, Acts 17:26, "And he made from one blood every nation of mankind to live on all the face of the earth." The white woman wrote down the references on a slip of paper, but didn't return. On Tuesday, the prisoners were hauled before court for a show trial. Without representation and with some of the same men who beat them acting as jurors, they were found guilty of disturbing the peace and resisting arrest. FBI agents, thanks to calls and telegrams to Attorney General Robert Kennedy, and J. Edgar Hoover, sent by civil rights activist Julian Bond and SNCC staff, eventually conducted a cursory investigation. On Wednesday Bevel, accompanied by Andrew Young and Cotton, finally got them released on bond. Their relief was quickly dashed by the devastating news that Medgar Evers, the field secretary for the NAACP, had been shot in the back and killed outside his home in Jackson, Mississippi.

Hamer was taken first to a nearby hospital in Greenwood and then to Atlanta for more extensive medical care paid for by the SCLC. She then traveled to Washington, DC, and New York City, staying away from home for a month, refusing visits from her family, except for one sister, to keep them from seeing her bruised and battered condition, and probably to recover emotionally from the physical and sexual violence she had endured. In fall 1963, she spoke at a Freedom Vote rally in Greenwood, urging her fellow Mississippians to participate in the Freedom Vote, basing her rhetoric on the Bible, hymns, and preaching of her and their black church background:

> From the fourth chapter of St. Luke beginning at the eighteenth verse: "The Spirit of the Lord is upon me because he has anointed me to preach the gospel to the poor. He has sent me to heal the brokenhearted, to preach deliverance to the captive, and recover the sight to the blind, to set at liberty to them who are bruised, to preach the acceptable year of the Lord." Now the time have come that was Christ's purpose on earth. And we only been getting by, by paying our way to Hell. But the time is out. When Simon Cryrene was helping Christ to bear his cross up the hill, he said "Must Jesus bear this cross alone? And all the world go free?" He said, "No, there's a cross for everyone and there's a cross for me. This consecrated cross I'll bear, till death shall set me free. And then go home a crown to wear, for there's a crown for me."
>
> And it's no easy way out. We just got to wake up and face it, folks. And if I can face the issue, you can too. . . . But you see, it's poison, it's poison for us not to speak what we know is right. As Christ said from the seventeenth chapter of Acts

and the twenty-sixth verse says: "has made of one blood all nations, for to dwell on the face of the earth." Then it's no different, we just have different color.

And brother . . . I been sick of this system as long as I can remember. . . . I been as hungry—it's a funny thing since I started working for Christ—it's kind of like in the twenty-third of Psalms when he says, "Thou prepareth a table before me in the presence my enemies. Thou anointed my head with oil and my cup runneth over."

So long as you know you going for something, you put up a life. That it can be like Paul, say "I fought a good fight." And I've "kept the faith." You know, it had been a long time—people, I have worked, I have worked as hard as anybody. I have been picking cotton and would be so hungry—and . . . wondering what I was going to cook that night. But you see all of them things was wrong, you see? And I have asked God, I said, "Now Lord"—and you have too—ain't no need to lie and say that you ain't. Said, "Open a way for us." Said, "Please make a way for us, Jesus." Said, "Where I can stand up and speak for my race and speak for these hungry children." And he opened a way and all of them mostly backing out.

You see, he made it so plain for us. He sent a man in Mississippi with same name that Moses had to go to Egypt. And tell him to go down in Mississippi and tell [Governor] Ross Barnett to let my people go. And you know I feel good, I feel good. I never know today what's going to happen to me tonight, but I do know as I walk alone, I walk with my hand in God's hand. . . .

All we got to do—that's why I love the song "This Little Light of Mine" from the fifth chapter of Matthew. He said: "A city that's set on a hill cannot be hid." And I don't mind my light shining. I don't hide that I'm fighting for freedom because Christ died to set us free. And he stayed here until he got thirty-three years old, letting us know how we would have to walk.[12]

This passage illustrates the power of Hamer's eloquence, with its seamless connection of scriptural interpretation to the experience of poor, rural, black Mississippians like herself, demonstrating the mighty acts of God within their own lives, and so grounding their hope and courage in God's active presence in their time and place to deliver them from bondage in the Egypt of Mississippi. The witty aptness of her comment on Bob Moses's surname makes an old and profound allusion to the African American spiritual "Go Down Moses," with all the historic resonance it carried for her audience/congregation.

In September 1964, she delivered a speech before a mass meeting assembled in Indianola. Describing in detail her experience in Winona for the first time publicly, she claimed that just as God had delivered the three Hebrew children, Shadrach, Meshach, and Abednego, from the fiery furnace of old, so had he freed his three children, Hamer, Ponder, and Guyot, from that Mississippi jail. The preachers preached about this text, she observed, but they had lived it. In brief, God was acting in Mississippi as he had in Babylon to save his people. And repeating the line from her Greenwood sermon, she made it plain that now was the time of God's liberation from the Egypt of Mississippi. She identified the situation of black Mississippians along with their duty to stand up and register to vote with the demands of Jesus in the Sermon on the Mount:

> He said, "Blessed are ye when men shall revile you and prosecute you, and shall set almighty evil against you falsely for my sake. Rejoice and be exceedingly glad, for great is your reward in heaven. For, so they prosecuted the prophets which

were before you." That's why I tell you tonight that you have a responsibility. And if you plan to walk in Christ's footstep and keep his commandments, you are willing to launch out unto the deep and go the courthouse, not come here tonight to see what I look like, but to do something about the system here. We are not . . . fighting to save these people because we hate 'em, but we are fighting these people because we love 'em and we are the only thing can save 'em now. We are fighting to save these people from their hate and from all the things that would be so bad against them. We want them to see the right way.

Every night of my life that I lay down, before I go to sleep, I pray for these people that despitefully use me. And Christ said, "The meek shall inherit the earth." And he said before one tenth of one dot of his word would fail, heaven and earth would pass away, but his word would stand forever. And I believe tonight that one day in Mississippi, if I have to die for this, we shall overcome. "We shall overcome," means something to me tonight. . . . And one day, by standin' up, goin' to the courthouse try to register and vote, that we get people this concerned about us.[13]

Despite Hamer's account, the testimony of her seven jail companions as well as that of the two prisoners forced to beat them, and the FBI special agents who visited their cells, the all-white jury of men assembled in federal court in Oxford, Mississippi, from December 2–6, 1963, took seventy-five minutes to find the policemen "not guilty" of all charges brought against them. Rather than dissuading Hamer from further civil rights activism, the Winona torture reinforced her commitment to work for political change through increasing black voter registration and local Freedom School education: "If them crackers in Winona thought they'd discouraged me from fighting, I guess they found out different.

I'm going to stay in Mississippi and if they shoot me down, I'll be buried here. I don't want equal rights with the white man. . . . We have to build our own power. We have to win every single political office we can, where we have a majority of black people."[14] Three months after the Winona verdict, on the evening of March 20, 1964, she announced her candidacy for the US Congress to represent the second congressional district of Mississippi, which included the twenty-four counties that made up the Delta region and constituted the largest district in the state. The last black person to represent this overwhelmingly black district was John R. Lynch during Reconstruction. In 1964, African Americans made up 59 percent of the district but only a small percentage of the registered voters. For example, in Sunflower County, 51 percent of voting-age whites were registered compared to only 0.9 percent of the black voting-age population. Hamer was also the first black woman to run for Congress in Mississippi. Her opponent, Jamie Whitten, had held the seat since 1941 and had positions on influential congressional committees. On voting day, June 2, 1964, Hamer cast the first vote of her life. And it was for herself. The official count gave Whitten the election, 35,218 to her 621, but there was no way to verify the accuracy of the count without federal examiners or neutral observers. Two weeks later, she went to Washington, DC, to testify about racial discrimination in Mississippi at a hearing organized by COFO before a panel of distinguished scholars, writers, and journalists, which issued a report read into the *Congressional Record*. A national spotlight was approaching the darkness of Mississippi.

Given the small gains in increasing black voter registration, COFO leaders in 1962 had decided to launch a Freedom Vote project for the fall 1963 election in order to counter segregationist claims that blacks were not interested in voting and offer practice to those who had never had the opportunity to cast a ballot. The Freedom Party welcomed whites as well as blacks and exemplified the fact by nominating for governor Aaron Henry, a black pharmacist from Clarksdale and chair of COFO, and Edwin King, a white chaplain at Tougaloo College, for lieutenant governor. To get out the vote, Moses with the help of Stanford professor Allard Lowenstein developed a plan to recruit Stanford and Yale students to spend two weeks in Mississippi helping spread the canvas effort. Lowenstein, an active opponent of South African apartheid, had learned about organizing mock elections from visiting that country. In spite of arrests and beatings, the students did door-to-door canvasing in black neighborhoods. On Election Day, 93,000 votes were cast at tables set up in barbershops and beauty parlors as well as on sidewalks. Henry and King won easily.

Spurred by the success of the Freedom Vote project and in order to increase national awareness of the racial situation in Mississippi, COFO leaders decided to organize a campaign to recruit a much larger group of college students from around the nation to spend the entire summer of 1964 in Mississippi canvasing black residents to vote, teaching children in Freedom Schools, establishing community centers, and living spread out within the homes of the state's impoverished black communities. Posters and announcements were spread on campuses nationwide to advertise and attract interested students, and orientation and training sessions were conducted at Western College for Women in Oxford, Ohio. A total of 900 volunteers, of whom 135 were African Americans, attended the two sessions. Eventually around 1,000 volunteers, including lawyers, doctors, and psychotherapists, traveled to Mississippi for Freedom Summer. The first training session focused on community canvasing, and the second on teaching the Freedom Schools. Hamer supported the project from the start and attended the second session, held June 22–27, 1964. There she impressed the students with her singing, and moved them with the authenticity of her rendition of the deep longing expressed in "Oh Freedom" and the determined faith of "We Shall Not Be Moved." She also warned them not to scorn religion: "Our religion is very important to us—you'll have to understand that."[15] And she taught them the lesson she had learned from her mother: the futility of hatred—a lesson reinforced by Christianity. "Ain't no such a thing as I can hate and hope to see God's face." "Help us communicate with white people. Regardless of what they act like, there's some good there. How can we say we love God and hate our brothers and sisters? We got to reach them; if only the people coming down can help us reach them." This faith was about to be sorely tested. On June 20, the first 200 volunteers left for Mississippi. The next day news arrived that three civil rights workers—Andrew Goodman, a student volunteer who had attended the first session, Michael (Mickey) Schwerner, a CORE organizer in Meridien, Mississippi, and CORE worker James Chaney, a black Mississippi native—had disappeared while investigating the bombing of a black Methodist church in Longdale, Mississippi. Their disappearance focused the attention of the national press on the state. Rita Schwerner, Mickey's wife and fellow CORE activist, was training volunteers when she heard the news, and remarked, "It's tragic that white northerners have to be caught up in the machinery of injustice and indifference in the South before the American people register concern. I personally suspect that if Mr. Chaney, who is a native Mississippian, had been alone at the time of the disappearance, that this case, like so many others . . . would have gone completely unnoticed." In August, their bodies were found buried in an earthen dam near Philadelphia, Mississippi.[16] The three families wanted them to be buried next to each other, but the segregation laws of Mississippi prohibited even integration of the dead, so Chaney was buried in a black cemetery.

While she could be critical of the unthinking behavior of some of the Freedom Summer volunteers, particularly the young white women who socialized publicly with young black men and acted too casually in an atmosphere of extreme danger, Hamer credited them with the dawning of a new day in Mississippi:

> Although they were strangers, they were the best friend we ever met. This was the beginning of the New Kingdom in Mississippi . . . They did something in Mississippi that gave us the hope that we had prayed for for so many years. We had wondered if there was anybody human enough to see us as human beings instead of animals. These young people were so Christlike! James Chaney, Andrew Goodman, and Michael Schwerner gave their lives that one day we would be free. . . . Not only did it have an effect on the black people of Mississippi but it touched some of the white people who don't yet dare speak out."[17]

One of the most important results of the student volunteers' efforts was the establishment of the Mississippi Freedom Democratic Party (MFDP) as a legally constituted political party to challenge the regular Mississippi Democratic Party with its policy of excluding black membership. By the end of August 1964, eighty thousand blacks, thanks to student canvasing, had joined the MFDP. That same month, the party held its first state convention at the Masonic Temple in Jackson, attracting a crowd of twenty-five hundred. The participants selected a delegation of sixty-four blacks and four whites to challenge the seating of the all-white regular party at the Democratic National Convention in Atlantic City, New Jersey. Henry, Hamer, Victoria Gray, Ed King, and Annie Devine were selected to lead the delegation. Though their challenge would ultimately fail, due to the intense political pressure that Lyndon Baines Johnson exerted on the national Democratic Party's Credentials Committee, the MFDP's presence would attract the attention of the television media and catapult Hamer vividly onto the national scene. Testifying before the committee on the first day of the convention and before a live television feed, Hamer spoke about her attempt to register to vote and being fired as a result, and the brutal beatings she had endured in the Winona jail for attending a civil rights meeting: "They beat me and they beat me with the long, flat blackjack. I screamed to God in pain. My dress worked itself up. I tried to pull it down. And a policeman pulled it back up." She concluded, "All of this is on account of we want to register, to become first-class citizens. If the Freedom Democratic Party is not seated now, I question America. The land of the free and the home of the brave? Where we have to sleep with our telephones off the hook, because our lives be threatened daily? Because we want to live as decent human beings in America. Thank you."[18]

Watching her testimony on television, an angry Johnson quickly called an impromptu news conference to distract attention from "that illiterate woman," as he later characterized her. But his strategy backfired as the national networks replayed her testimony in full on the evening news. The committee was bombarded by telegrams and phone calls from around the country from viewers moved by compassion, outrage, and shame to support seating the MFDP delegation. Despite the sympathy of some of the committee members, not enough voted to seat the MFDP delegates. Johnson had ordered Senator Hubert H. Humphrey (accompanied by well-known liberals Walter Mondale and Walter Reuther) to arrange a compromise that would give the MFDP two non-voting seats. But when Humphrey outlined the compromise, pleading that his position on the ticket was at stake, Hamer responded:

> Senator Humphrey, I been praying about you, and I been thinking about you, and you're a good man, and you know what's right. The trouble is, you're afraid to do what you know is right. You just want this job. I lost my job. Do you mean to tell me that your position is more important than four hundred thousand black people's lives? Senator Humphrey, I know lots of people in Mississippi who have lost their jobs trying to register to vote. I had to leave the plantation where I worked in Sunflower County, Mississippi. Now if you lose this job of Vice-President because you do what is right, because you help the MFDP, everything will be all right. God will take care of you. But if you take this job, why, you will never be able to do any good for civil rights, for poor people, for peace, or any of those things you talk about. Senator Humphrey, I'm going to pray to Jesus for you.[19]

After heated discussion, the group rejected the offer, contrary to the advice of Martin Luther King Jr., Bayard Rustin, and a patronizing Roy Wilkins, executive secretary of the NAACP, all of whom defended the compromise as a "symbolic victory." As Hamer put it, "We didn't come all this way for no two seats." Meanwhile, all but three of the regular Mississippi delegation abandoned the convention rather than swear allegiance to the party ticket and platform. With credentials given them by friendly delegates from other states, several of the MFDP delegates, including Hamer, attempted to take the empty seats but were ousted by security guards—as the whole scene was captured on live television.[20]

Exhausted and chastened by the encounter with the machinations of national politics, Hamer and ten other SNCC leaders were treated to a memorable three-week trip to West Africa by singer and social activist Harry Belafonte, who recognized their burnout. In later interviews, Hamer recalled it as a deeply moving and profoundly enlightening experience, wiping away years of racist stereotypes:

> Being from the South we never was taught much about our African heritage. The way everybody talked to us, everybody in Africa was savages and really stupid people. But I've seen more savage white folks here in America than I seen in Africa. I saw black men flying the airplanes, driving buses, sitting behind the big desks in the bank and just doing everything that I was used to seeing white people do. I saw for the first time in my life a black stewardess walking through the plane and that was quite an inspiration for me.
>
> I wasn't in Guinea more than a couple of hours before President [Ahmed Sékou] Touré came to see us. And I just compared my feelings. I've tried so hard so many times to see the president in this country and I wasn't given that chance. But the president over there cared enough to visit us. He invited us to his palace and that was the first time I'd ever had a chance to go in a palace. I just thought it was great to see African people so kind. It was so vice-versa what I'd heard that I couldn't hardly believe it.

Belafonte later explained the poignancy of the moment when Hamer met Touré:

> She stopped dead when she saw Sékou Touré, in his white fez and white robes, flashing a grin of welcome at her. He came over, kissed her on each cheek, and said how pleased he was to meet her. With that, Fannie threw her arms around him,

buried her face in his chest, and wept. I understood completely. Neither Fannie nor any of the others had ever seen a black head of state. The very idea, after enduring beatings and police dogs and constant oppression by the only authority figures they knew—white ones—was overwhelming. To these bone-tired activists, Sékou Touré was a symbol of true freedom and self-rule. To have him . . . say "Welcome home"—it was no wonder Fannie dissolved in tears.[21]

When Congress convened in 1965, the winners in the second Freedom Election, Hamer, Gray, and Devine, lead a sustained effort to unseat the five newly elected Mississippi congressmen, as illegally elected due to widespread suppression of the black vote in violation of the Fifteenth Amendment to the Constitution. Mountains of evidence of voter fraud and intimidation were collected amounting to ten thousand pages of affidavits from six hundred witnesses to that effect. The House of Representatives rejected the challenge by a vote of 228 to 143 with 51 abstentions and 10 voting present. Interviewed about the results, Hamer broke down in tears and then asked, "What kind of country is it that is afraid to let the people know the truth? I'm not crying for myself today, but I'm crying for America. I cry that the Constitution of the United States, written down on paper, applies only to white people. But we will come back year after year until we are allowed our rights as citizens. . . . It ain't over yet. We're coming back here, again, and again and again."[22] Ironically, as Hamer remarked later, Lynch had won his challenge to be seated a century earlier; so much for progress.

While still working for black political participation and impartial voter registration, she turned more and more to the needs of the local black poor for decent housing, adequate food, and access to health care. Moreover, she and Pap suddenly had two babies to care for. Tragically, their twenty-two-year-old adopted daughter Dorothy Jean, who had two small children and a husband on active duty in Vietnam, suffered from malnutrition and had grown so weak that Hamer took her to the local hospital, where she was denied admission because of race. Another hospital also refused to admit her. Finally, Hamer found a hospital that would accept her daughter, in Memphis, 119 miles away. Dorothy died in her mother's arms of cerebral hemorrhage at the hospital entrance.

In 1969, Hamer began to organize a program that became the Freedom Farm Cooperative. She started with a small but ingenuous project, "the pig bank." The local chapter of the National Council of Negro Women initiated the effort by donating 50 pigs to the Freedom Farm. Any family was eligible to receive a pregnant pig, resulting in 9 to 20 piglets. When two sows from that litter became pregnant, the family had to donate them to another needy family. After the first year, around 135 families received pigs. By the third year, over 300 families had benefited from the bank, and between 2,000 and 3,000 new pigs had been born. By 1973, some 900 families had participated in the program. The Freedom Farm also invested in acquiring land for growing vegetables and small amounts of cotton. By 1971, there were 33 plots of land, totaling 1,940 acres owned by black Sunflower County residents, comprising almost 33 percent of the black-owned land in the county. By 1972, the Freedom Farm had constructed 70 affordable houses, including the home that Hamer lived in with her family for the rest of her life.[23] These houses had the "luxury" of paved streets, running water, plumbing, and indoor toilets.

Her efforts to help local Mississippians socially and economically through the Freedom Farm cooperative project involved her in extensive fund-raising travel to lecture around the country, adding to the number of engagements that her national political notoriety had already attracted. The offers for speaking appearances extended far and wide, including Williams Institutional CME Church in Harlem alongside Malcolm X; the Vietnam War moratorium rally in Berkeley, California; Loop College in Chicago; the University of Wisconsin at Madison; the National Women's Political Caucus in Washington, DC; Harvard University in Cambridge, Massachusetts; Duke University in Durham, North Carolina; Carleton College in Northfield, Minnesota; San Jose, California; Norwalk, Connecticut; Seattle, Washington; Omaha, Nebraska; and appearances on both the David Frost and Phil Donahue television shows as well as numerous radio interviews. Wherever she went, her audiences were moved by her story and the power of her voice, whose effectiveness arose from the soil and bloody history of poor black people in Mississippi, a voice honed in the tones and cadences of the black Baptist church and the music that arose therein, a voice that drew instinctively on the biblical stories and prophetic texts that anointed her "to speak deliverance to those held in bondage" by racism in this nation, white as well as black. The power of her voice arose from its unimpeachable authenticity, from one who all her life had been scorned and "buked" within the prison of American apartheid, a hundred years after slavery. Hamer did not just condemn racism and poverty; she herself suffered racism and endured poverty. She did not just speak *for* the local people; she embodied the voice of the local people, and bore the scars to show for it.

Speaking before an audience at Loop College in Chicago in May 1970, she diagnosed the sickness of the United States:

> I've seen what hate, and we all see what hate, is doing to this whole sick country at this moment. America is a sick place, and man is on the critical list. But we are determined to bring a

change not only for ourselves, but I believe that we are some of God's chosen people, you know a lot of folks say, "Well, I don't believe in God," but the reason they said, they see so much hypocrisy in the churches. But I believe in God and I believe in the beautiful passage of the fortieth chapter of Isaiah and the fourth verse that says, "The valley will be exalted"—and that's people. "The mountains and the hills would be made level, and the crooked roads be made straight." We tried to go from the level of voter registration and getting people registered—and I want to tell you something about this county I'm from. It's what you call the ruralest of the ruralest, poorest of the poorest, U.S.A. This is the home of Senator James O. Eastland that in 1967 received $255,000 to let his land waste, while people on the plantation suffered from malnutrition. So this is a sickness that's not only occurring in Mississippi, because you have a hell of a lot of problems in Chicago. . . . We are going to make things better, and we are going to straighten out the crooked roadways, not only in Mississippi, but throughout this country. As I close I always like to think about a song my mother used to sing a song, it was a hymn that said, "Should earth against my soul engage, and fiery darts be hurled, when I can smile at Satan's rage, and face this frowning world."[24]

In one of several speeches she gave in Madison, Wisconsin, to raise funds for the Freedom Farm Cooperative, Hamer focused on the interrelationship of all classes and races:

And we plan to make this a better place for all the citizens, both black, red, whites, and browns and we want you to understand this I never been hung up in all of my work in that because I know that a lot of black people have given their lives. But I also know it was people like Andy Goodman,

Michael Schwerner, and James Chaney that gave their lives in the state of Mississippi so that all of us would have a better chance. And when they died there they didn't just die for me, but they died for you because your freedom is shackled in chains to mine. And until I am free, you are not free either. And if you think you are free, you drive down to Mississippi with your Wisconsin license plate and you will see what I am talking about. . . . And you don't tell me that you can't change a man's mind by not hating. We have gone through all kinds of pressure, but I refuse to hate a man because he hate me. Because if I hate you because you hate me, it's no different both of us are miserable. And we going to finally have something in common: hating. But as a result of what I can give of myself that I can love you if you hate me, we have poor whites that's coming into this organization and we're going to feed not only the black people of Sunflower County, but all of the people that's hungry regardless of color.[25]

Earlier than King, Hamer began to speak out against the Vietnam War, in 1965 at a demonstration in Lafayette Park across from the White House, after she sent a telegram to President Johnson "telling him to bring the people home from the Dominican Republic and Vietnam where they have no business anyhow, and bring them to Mississippi and Louisiana because if this is a Great Society, I'd hate to see a bad one." "But at that time," she told a crowd gathered in Berkeley for a Vietnam War moratorium rally in October 1969, "we felt very alone because when we start saying the war is wrong in Vietnam, well people looked at us like we were something out of space. . . . [I]f you are right you have to stand on that principle and if it's necessary to die on the principle because I am sick of the racist war in Vietnam when we don't have justice in the United States."[26]

In the fall 1968 issue of the liberal journal *Katallagete*, she expanded on her criticism of the church's failure on issues of race:

Just as it's time for America to wake up, it is long past time for the churches to wake up. The churches have got to say that they will have no more talk that "because your skin is a little different, you're better than they are." The churches have got to remember how Christ dealt with the poor people, in the 4th chapter of St. Luke, and the 18th verse, when he said, "The spirit of the Lord is upon me, because he hath anointed me to preach the gospel to the poor; he hath sent me to heal the brokenhearted, to preach deliverance to the captives, and recovering of sight to the blind to set at liberty them that are bruised." Because Jesus wasn't just talking about black people, or about white people, he was talking about people. There's no difference in people, for in the 17th chapter of the Book of Acts, the 26th verse, Paul says "God hath made of one blood all nations of men for to dwell on all the face of the earth." That means that whether we're white, black, red, yellow or polka dot, we're made from the same blood. . . . We have to realize just how grave the problem is in the United States today, and I think the 6th chapter of Ephesians, the 11th and 12th verses helps us to know how grave the problem is, and what it is we are up against. It says: "Put on the whole armor of God that ye may be able to stand against the wiles of the devil. For we wrestle not against flesh and blood, but against principalities, against powers, against the rulers of the darkness of this world, against spiritual wickedness in high places." This is what I think about when I think of my own work in the fight for freedom, because before 1962, I would have been afraid to have spoken before more than six people. Since that time I have had to speak before thousands in the fight for freedom, and I believe that God gave me the strength to be able to speak in this cause."[27]

In winter 1975, her health began to fail. She continued to work on ensuring that the MFDP sent an integrated delegation to the Chicago Democratic Convention in 1976. Early in 1977, she entered the Mound Bayou Community Hospital suffering from diabetes, heart disease, and cancer. In constant pain, she felt depressed and abandoned. On March 14, she died of heart failure, at the age of sixty. She died penniless.

Owen Brooks, a black activist from Boston who moved to Mississippi to organize farm cooperatives, raised the money for her funeral arrangements. Hundreds of local people gathered to pay their last respects at Williams Chapel Missionary Baptist Church, where fifteen years earlier, Hamer had first volunteered to register to vote. They heard eulogies by Bond, John Lewis, Stokely Carmichael, Henry, and Andrew Young, who finished by leading the crowd in singing "This Little Light of Mine." Two days after her death, the Mississippi legislature unanimously passed a resolution praising her service to the state. In 2012, a memorial garden, recreation center, and eight-foot statue were dedicated to keeping the memory of Hamer alive.[28]

In a conversation with McLaurin shortly before her death, Hamer said, "Mac, we ain't free yet. The kids need to know their mission." Surely, working to achieve that mission would be her preferred memorial. Reflecting on the power of her speaking, Congresswoman Eleanor Holmes Norton claimed that she had no equal except for King. Hamer had

the capacity to put together a mosaic of coherent thought about freedom and justice, so that when it was all through, you knew what you had heard because it held together with wonderful cohesion. . . . She also . . . would break out into song at the end of her things, and I'm telling you, you've never heard a room flying [like one] that Fannie Lou Hamer set afire. . . . She has put her finger on something truly important that all of us had felt but she had said. You heard that all the time. What really gets you is that person somehow concretizes an idea that you had never quite been able to fully form. And she did that in this extraordinary ringing style and then ended up singing "This Little Light of Mine." You never needed to hear anybody else speak again. . . . I'm convinced she chose that song for a reason . . . that she knew that [it] summarized her life.[29]

Hamer's voice rang with authenticity, a moral authority that can only come from suffering. It was this religious authenticity and authority that gave such deep resonance to her voice, as it had to the voices of her slave ancestors and their descendants down all the long years of hoping and toiling for freedom.

⌒ AFTERWORD ⌒

> Which of these three, do you think, proved to be a
> neighbor to the man who fell among the robbers? He
> said, "The one who showed him mercy." And Jesus
> said to him, "You go, and do likewise."
>
> —Luke 10:36–37

As I WRITE, THE RECENT MURDER OF NINE BLACK PEOPLE attending an evening Bible study class at the historic Emanuel African Methodist Episcopal Church in Charleston, South Carolina, on June 17, 2015, has focused national attention on racism, already roiled by a succession of police killings of unarmed black men, captured on cell phone videos. The pastor and state senator Reverend Clementa C. Pinckney (age forty-one), Cynthia Marie Graham Hurd (age fifty-four), Susie Jackson (age eighty-seven), Ethel Lee Lance (age seventy), Depayne Middleton-Doctor (age forty-nine), Tywanza Sanders (age twenty-six), Daniel Simmons Sr. (age seventy-four), Sharonda Coleman-Singleton (age forty-five), and Myra Thompson (age fifty-nine) were shot to death by a twenty-one-year-old white supremacist, Dylan Roof, who hoped to cause a race war. He had chosen the church after research informed him of its significant history. The site of a planned slave rebellion led by a free black, Denmark Vesey, the church had been raised to the ground after the plot was discovered, and its leaders deported or executed in 1822. Ironically, after the

Civil War, the church was rebuilt according to the architectural plans of Vesey's son. The televised eulogy for the slain pastor was delivered by President Barack Obama, who surprised and moved many viewers by leading the congregation in singing "Amazing Grace," the hymn written by John Newton, a former slave ship captain after his conversion to Christianity. As the president emphasized, family members of some of the victims amazed many by expressing their forgiveness to the killer during his arraignment—a gesture in imitation of Christ on the cross that Fannie Lou Hamer and Annelle Ponder would have surely approved. From the celebration of the anniversary of the Selma march to the mourning at Charleston in less than a year: Was it a cycle of stasis or change, despair or hope? Surely the prophetic voices described in this book would counsel against the paralysis of despair by urging action. In times as bleak as any, they kept their hope alive by speaking and acting against the giant triplets of racism, militarism, and materialism that dominate contemporary society. They kept hope alive by repeating the biblical narratives of Exodus, identifying God's liberation of his people from slavery with their own struggle for freedom. They kept hope alive by repeating the words of the prophets of ancient Israel—Isaiah, Jeremiah, Ezekiel, and Amos—that motivated action by expressing God's pathos for suffering humanity as well as God's preference for social justice for the poor, the oppressed, the widow, the orphan, and the immigrant over the cultic piety supporting the status quo. They kept hope alive by troubling the consciences of their fellow citizens, shaming them out of the slumber of contentment and apathy of ease to act as if the proclamations of the prophets, the Sermon on the Mount, the Beatitudes, the Parables, and Matthew 25 constituted a charter for a society, consonant with the nation's founding principles of civil equality, justice, and liberty for all. "I question America. The land of the free and the home of the brave?" as Hamer so powerfully put it.

Moreover, they took sustenance from exemplary figures and saints who served as their models and ideals of thought and action—sources of emulation and identification. For several, such as Thomas Merton and Martin Luther King Jr., the examples of Henry David Thoreau and Mahatma Gandhi were important. For others, such as Howard Thurman and A. J. Muste, the influence of Rufus Jones and the Quaker witness was seminal. For Dorothy Day, who preferred to be a saint rather than to be called one, her mentor Peter Maurin and his exposition of Catholic social teaching was transformational, as was her devotion to individual saints like Saint Thérèse of Lisieux, Saint Martin de Porres, Saint Francis of Assisi, Saint Catherine of Siena, and others featured in the pages of the *Catholic Worker*. They constituted a "cloud of witnesses," supporting her dedication to the poor and the cause of peace. For Abraham Joshua Heschel, the holy rabbinic ancestors in his lineage combined with figures like Moses Maimonides and Albert Schweitzer to model a life of scholarship, mysticism, and social action. For Hamer, the courage of her mother, heroic example of Mississippi volunteers like Bob Moses, training she received from Septima Clark, and fellow activists in the voter registration campaign all served as exemplary figures.

Can the prophets depicted in this book act in turn as exemplary figures for us today? It is a question that readers will have to answer for themselves. It is not an easy question. It is one that I've wrestled with ever since I was seventeen and heard Day claim without hesitation that the United States ought to unilaterally disarm. As John W. O'Malley aptly observes in his book *Four Cultures of the West*, "Prophetic rhetoric provokes a crisis situation. By definition given to

confrontation, it forces choice." An uncomfortable but hopeful choice, he contends,

> Yet when the cause is just, nothing other than the inflated
> rhetoric of the prophet, it seems, can shock us out of our
> complacency, and shove before our eyes in all their starkness
> the alternatives we need to face. It forces us to confront them
> and to take a stand one way or the other. No wiggle [room].
> It also offers hope when the cause seems hopeless and when
> all the calculation has come to naught. It galvanizes us to ac-
> tion against seemingly insuperable odds because the proph-
> ets who wield this rhetoric have a dream that convey them
> and us to places where we otherwise would never have the
> courage to go.[1]

I conclude this book by returning to Selma and an incident that continues to haunt me as a poignant illustration
of the power of the divine pathos that motivated all of the
prophets I have discussed in its pages. For me it serves as a
simple yet powerful image of the compassion that energized
so many to participate in the civil rights movement—a compassion that Heschel identified with the divine pathos for humanity that burns like a fire in the prophet's bones. Attending the memorial service for James Reeb were two little girls,
Sheyann Webb (age eight) and Rachel West (age nine), who
participated prominently in the daily demonstrations. Years
later they recalled their responses to Reeb's death in Selma at
the hands of white supremacists. In West's words:

> Me and Sheyann used to walk about the church there and
> look for some sign that would tell us the Lord was on our
> side, that He was watching us. We'd look and we'd see a leaf
> falling, and we'd say that was the sign. And we'd know we
> were winning. We'd see the moon shining down some nights

and we'd say that was the sign. And we'd say we were winning. We'd hear the wind blowing or hear the thunder. That
was the sign, we'd say. We were winning. So this night, very
late, the night James Reeb died, we were out there with all
these sad people, and so many of them were still crying. So
we walked about the crowd looking for a sign, because we
needed that assurance. And we'd heard somebody—one of
the ministers or nuns—say that when a good person dies the
Lord hangs out a new star in the night. So we looked up for a
shiny new star . . . but the sky was full of clouds. And I said to
Sheyann, "There ain't no sign tonight." And she says, "Keep
lookin' Rachel, 'til we see it." So we kept standing there, with
our heads turned upward like that. And all of a sudden it
started raining . . . right in our faces. And I yelled, "Shey,
there ain't gonna be no sign." But she's still looking up like
that and all of a sudden she says, "The rain's the sign. The rain
is." And I looked up again, letting it just splatter all over my
face and in my eyes. The sudden way it had started made me
agree that it surely must be the sign. So we sat on the steps of
Brown Chapel . . . shivering and praying there. And we were
convinced that this rain meant that even the Lord in Heaven
was sad by James Reeb's death and He was joining us in our
sadness, in our weeping.[2]

⌒ NOTES ⌒

CHAPTER 1: ABRAHAM JOSHUA HESCHEL

1. Abraham Joshua Heschel, *Moral Grandeur and Spiritual Audacity: Essays*, edited by Susannah Heschel (New York: Farrar, Straus and Giroux, 1996), 384.

2. Ibid., ix. For more biographical details, see ibid., introduction.

3. Ibid., 392.

4. Ibid., 267

5. Abraham Joshua Heschel, *A Passion for Truth* (New York: Farrar, Straus and Giroux, 1973), xiii.

6. Robert McAfee Brown, "'Some Are Guilty, All Are Responsible': Heschel's Social Ethics," in *Abraham Joshua Heschel: Exploring His Life and Thought*, ed. John C. Merkle (New York: Macmillan, 1985), 129, citing Abraham Joshua Heschel, *The Earth Is the Lord's* (New York: Henry Shuman, 1950), 72.

7. For information about Heschel's biography, I've found the short summary by Susannah Heschel to be helpful. See her introduction to Heschel, *Moral Grandeur and Spiritual Audacity*, vi–xxx. For a detailed account, see Edward Kaplan and Samuel H. Dressner, *Abraham Joshua Heschel: Prophetic Witness*, 2 vols. (New Haven, CT: Yale University Press, 1998); Edward Kaplan, *Spiritual Radical: Abraham Joshua Heschel in America, 1940–1972* (New Haven, CT: Yale University Press, 2007). Among the many books on Heschel's thought, for an especially perceptive and thorough one, see Shai Held, *Abraham Joshua Heschel: The Call of Transcendence* (Bloomington: Indiana University Press, 2013).

8. Abraham Joshua Heschel, *The Ineffable Name of God: Man—Poems*, translated by Morton M. Leifman, introduction by Edward K. Kaplan (New York: Continuum, 2004), 12, 43, 57. For a free translation of the poems, see Zalman M. Schachter-Shalomi, *Human: God's Ineffable Name* (Boulder, CO: Albion-Andalus Books, 2012).

9. Heschel, *Moral Grandeur*, 235.

10. Ibid., xxii–xxiii.

11. Abraham Joshua Heschel, *The Prophets* (New York: Perennial Classics, 2001), xxii. All citations are from this edition.

12. Ibid., 288–89.

13. Ibid., 292.

14. Samuel H. Dresner, "Heschel the Man," in *Abraham Joshua Heschel: Exploring His Life and Thought*, ed. John C. Merkle (New York: Macmillan, 1985), 21.

15. Robert McAfee Brown, "'Some Are Guilty, All Are Responsible': Heschel's Social Ethics," *Abraham Joshua Heschel: Exploring His Life and Thought*, ed. John C. Merkle (New York: Macmillan, 1985), 128, citing Abraham Joshua Heschel, *The Insecurity of Freedom: Essays on Human Existence* (New York: Noonday Press, 1967), 95.

16. Mathew Ahmann, ed., *Race: Challenge to Religion* (Chicago: Henry Regnery, 1963), 68.

17. Ibid., 58.

18. Ibid., 59.

19. Ibid., 67.

20. Ibid., 70–71.

21. Heschel, *Moral Grandeur*, xxiii–xxiv.

22. Kaplan, *Spiritual Radical*, 324–25.

23. Susannah Heschel, ed., *Abraham Joshua Heschel: Essential Writings* (Maryknoll, NY: Orbis Press, 2011), 83–84.

24. Cited in Michael A. Chester, *Divine Pathos and Human Being: The Theology of Abraham Joshua Heschel* (London: Vallentine Mitchell, 2005), 23.

25. See Susannah Heschel, "Theological Affinities in the Writings of Abraham Joshua Heschel and Martin Luther King, Jr.," *Conservative Judaism* 50, nos. 2–3 (1998): 126–43.

26. Cited in Donald Grayston and Michael W. Higgins, eds., *Thomas Merton: Pilgrim in Process* (Toronto: Griffin House, 1983), 98.

27. Thomas Merton, *Turning toward The World: The Pivotal Years; The Journals of Thomas Merton, Volume 4, 1960–1963* (New York: HarperCollins, 1966), 61–62.

28. Kaplan, *Spiritual Radical*, 256–57; entry on Judaism in William H. Shannon, Christine M. Bochen, and Patrick F. O'Connell, eds., *The Thomas Merton Encyclopedia* (Maryknoll, NY: Orbis Books, 1970), 234; Brenda Fish Faraday, "Thomas Merton's Prophetic Voice: Merton, Heschel, and Vatican II," in *Merton and Judaism*, ed. Beatrice Bruteau (Louisville, KY: Fons Vitae, 2003), 272–73. This book contains the successive versions of *Nostra Aetate* in appendix A, 341–71.

29. Abraham Joshua Heschel, "The Moral Outrage of Vietnam," in *Vietnam: Crisis of Conscience*, ed. Robert McAfee Brown, Abraham Joshua Heschel, and Michael Novak (New York: Association Press, 1967), 48–49; Samuel Dresner, "Abraham Joshua Heschel Ten Years after His Death," *Conservative Judaism* 36, no. 2 (Winter 1982–83): 5.

30. Cited in Heschel, *Abraham Joshua Heschel: Essential Writing*, 82–83.

31. Cited in John C. Merkle, ed., *Abraham Joshua Heschel: Exploring His Life and Thought* (New York: Macmillan, 1985), 134.

32. Susannah Heschel, "Heschel as Mensch: Testimony of His Daughter," *To Grow in Wisdom: An Anthology of Abraham Joshua Heschel*, ed. Jacob Neusner with Moam M. M. Neusner (New York: Madison Books, 1990), 205.

33. Heschel, *Moral Grandeur*, 262–63.

34. Television interview recorded with Carl Stern for the Eternal Light program produced by the Jewish Theological Seminary, broadcast February 4, 1973; for the transcript, see Heschel, *Moral Grandeur*, 395–412.

CHAPTER 2: A. J. MUSTE

1. Nat Hentoff, ed., *The Essays of A. J. Muste*, 2nd ed. (New York: A. J. Muste Memorial Institute, 2001), 284. For the entire essay, see ibid., 269–84. For Muste's autobiographical reflections, "Sketches for an Autobiography," which first appeared in the journal he coedited, *Liberation*, see ibid., 1–167. Hentoff, a journalist, expanded his *New Yorker* magazine profile of Muste into a book, *Peace Agitator: The Story of A. J. Muste* (New York: A. J. Muste Memorial Institute, 1963).

2. Jo Ann Ooiman Robinson, *Abraham Went Out: A Biography of A. J. Muste* (Philadelphia: Temple University Press, 1981), 3. Robinson's was the only scholarly biography of Muste until the publication of Leilah Danielson, *American Gandhi: A. J. Muste and the History of Radicalism in the Twentieth Century* (Philadelphia: University of Pennsylvania Press, 2014).

3. Cited in Hentoff, *Peace Agitator*, 27.

4. Hentoff, *Essays*, 22–23.

5. Danielson, *American Gandhi*, 31.

6. Cited in Hentoff, *Essays*, 36–37; Robinson, *Abraham Went Out*, 8–10.

7. Cited in Hentoff, *Essays*, 41–43.

8. Danielson, *American Gandhi*, 47.

9. Robinson, *Abraham Went Out*, 18.

10. Cited Hentoff, *Essays*, 44–46.

11. Rufus M. Jones, *The Social Law in the Spiritual World: Studies in Human and Divine Inter-Relationship* (Philadelphia: John C. Winston Co., 1904), 140.

12. Rufus M. Jones, *Studies in Mystical Religion* (London: Macmillan, 1909), xxxviii.

13. Robinson, 23; Hentoff, *Essays*, 55–56.

14. Robinson, *Abraham Went Out*, 22.

15. Cited in Hentoff, *Essays*, 77, 84, 142.

16. Robinson, *Abraham Went Out*, 39–40. For Dewey's comment and Robinson's evaluation of Muste's emotional reaction, see ibid., 48.

17. Cited Hentoff, *Essays*, 131.

18. Cited in ibid., 202–3.

19. Robinson, *Abraham Went Out*, 63–64.

20. Cited in Hentoff, *Peace Agitator*, 175. See also A. J. Muste, "The True International," in *The Essays of A. J. Muste*, ed. Nat Hentoff, 2nd ed. (New York: A. J. Muste Memorial Institute, 2001), 200–207.

21. Hentoff, *Peace Agitator*, 190–91.

22. Jo Ann Ooiman Robinson, "The Pharos of the East Side, 1937–1940: Labor Temple under the Direction of A. J. Muste," *Journal of Presbyterian History* 48, no. 1 (Spring 1970): 18–37, especially 22–23.

23. A. J. Muste, *Nonviolence in an Aggressive World* (New York: Harper and Brothers, 1940), 12–13.

24. Cited in Hentoff, *Peace Agitator*, 22.

25. Ibid., 23.

26. A. J. Muste, *Not by Might: Christianity, the Way to Human Decency* (New York: Harper and Brothers, 1947), 203.

27. Hentoff, *Essays*, 308.

28. "Speak Truth to Power: A Quaker Search for an Alternative to Violence," American Service Committee pamphlet, 1955, 70. A committee issued this pamphlet, but Muste was its primary author.

29. Muste, *Not by Might*, 46.

30. Ibid., 84–85.

31. Cited in Robinson, *Abraham Went Out*, 89, 90.

32. Muste, *Not by Might*, 169, 173.

33. Cited in Hentoff, *Peace Agitator*, 135.

34. Cited in Hentoff, *Essays*, 305n12.

35. Muste, *Not by Might*, 217.

36. Ibid., 219.

37. Robinson, *Abraham Went Out*, 159.

38. Larry Gara, introduction to *Peace Agitator: The Story of A. J. Muste*, by Nat Hentoff (New York: A. J. Muste Memorial Institute, 1963), i.

39. Dorothy Day, "On Pilgrimage—March 1964," *Catholic Worker*, 1, 2, 6.

40. Cited Hentoff, *Peace Agitator*, 155.

41. Cited Robinson, *Abraham Went Out*, 165–70.

42. Ibid., 137.

43. Ibid., 282n76.

44. Hentoff, *Peace Agitator*, 109–11.

45. Cited in ibid., 114.

46. Robinson, *Abraham Went Out*, 124–25. Muste's essay is reprinted in Hentoff, *Essays*, 409–20.

47. Cited in Hentoff, *Essays*, 88.

48. For a detailed account of this fascinating occasion, see Gordon Oyer, *Pursuing the Spiritual Roots of Protest* (Eugene, OR: Cascade Books), 167–92.

49. Hentoff, *Peace Agitator*, 111.

50. Larry Gara, cited in Hentoff, *Peace Agitator*, iii.

51. Cited in ibid., 11–12.

52. Robinson, *Abraham Went Out*, 206–8, 216–19.

53. Cited in *Catholic Worker*, February 1967, 2, 6, 7.

CHAPTER 3: DOROTHY DAY

1. Dorothy Day, *The Long Loneliness* (1952; repr., San Francisco: HarperCollins, 1997), 25.

2. Ibid., 28–29.

3. William D. Miller, *Dorothy Day: A Biography* (San Francisco: Harper and Row, 1984), 61. In addition to Day's *Long Loneliness* and Miller's biography, I have drawn from Jim Forest, *All Is Grace: A Biography of Dorothy Day* (Maryknoll, NY: Orbis Books, 2011) in this chapter. For past issues of the *Catholic Worker*, see http://www.catholicworker.org/ (accessed March 19, 2016).

4. Ibid., 179–81.

5. Ibid., 188.

6. William D. Miller, *All Is Grace: The Spirituality of Dorothy Day* (Garden City, NY: Doubleday, 1987), 62.

7. Dorothy Day, *Wisdom from Dorothy Day: A Radical Love*, ed. Patricia Miller (Frederick, MD: Word Among Us Press, 2000), 55–56.

8. Day, *Long Loneliness*, 140.

9. Ibid., 149–50.

10. Ibid., 164–66.

11. Miller, *Dorothy Day*, 237.

12. Cited in *Catholic Worker*, May 1977, 1, 9.

13. Dorothy Day, *The Duty of Delight: The Diaries of Dorothy Day*, ed. by Robert Ellsberg (Milwaukee: Marquette University Press, 2008), xv–xvi.

14. Dorothy Day, *On Pilgrimage* (Grand Rapids, MI: William B. Eerdmans Publishing Company, 1999), 24.

15. Cited in Miller, *Dorothy Day*, 259.

16. Day, *On Pilgrimage*, 24.

17. Cited in Dwight McDonald, "The Foolish Things of the World," *New Yorker*, October 4, 1952, 60.

18. Jim Forest, *Love Is the Measure: A Biography of Dorothy Day* (Mahwah, NJ: Paulist Press, 1986), 146.

19. William D. Miller, *All Is Grace: The Spirituality of Dorothy Day* (New York: Doubleday, 1987), 103–4.

20. Dorothy Day, *Loaves and Fishes* (1963; repr., Maryknoll, NY: Orbis Press, 1997), 87.

21. Mel Piehl, *Breaking Bread: The Catholic Worker and the Origin of Catholic Radicalism in America* (Philadelphia: Temple University Press, 1984), 99, 100; Dorothy Day, *From Union Square to Rome*, 2nd ed. (Maryknoll, NY: Orbis Books, 2006), 80.

22. Cited in Day, *Long Loneliness*, 80, 179.

23. William T. Cavanaugh, "Dorothy Day and the Mystical Body of Christ in the Second World War," in *Dorothy Day and the Catholic Worker Movement: Centenary Essays*, ed. William Thorn, Phillip Runkel, and Susan Mountin (Milwaukee: Marquette University Press, 2001), 463.

24. Dorothy Day, "On Pilgrimage," *Catholic Worker*, May 1948, 2.

25. Miller, *Dorothy Day*, 314–15, 331.

26. Miller, *Dorothy Day*, 331; Day, *Long Loneliness*, 181.

27. William D. Miller, *A Harsh and Dreadful Love: Dorothy Day and the Catholic Worker Movement* (New York: Image Books, 1974), 291–92.

28. Cited in *Catholic Worker*, November 1965.

29. Cited in *Catholic Worker*, May 1957; Miller, *Dorothy Day*, 441.

30. Cited in McDonald, "Foolish Things of the World," 54.

31. Barack Obama, *The Audacity of Hope* (New York: Crown Publishers, 2006), 218.

32. See the extended article on Plowshares in the March 9, 2015, issue of the *New Yorker*.

33. Miller, *Dorothy Day*, 261.

34. Ibid.; Day, *Long Loneliness*, 189, 236, 243.

CHAPTER 4: HOWARD THURMAN

1. Several important analyses of Thurman's life and thought have been written. In my view, the most helpful include Walter E. Fluker, *They Looked for a City: A Comparative Analysis of the Ideal of Community in the Thought of Howard Thurman and Martin Luther King, Jr.* (New York: University Press of America, 1989); Alonzo Johnson, *Good News for the Disinherited: Howard Thurman on Jesus of Nazareth and Human Liberation* (New York: University Press of America, 1997); Mozella G. Mitchell, ed., *The Human Search: Howard Thurman and the Quest for Freedom, Proceed-*

ings of the Second Annual Thurman Convocation (New York: Peter Lang, 1992); Alton B. Pollard III, *Mysticism and Social Change: The Social Witness of Howard Thurman* (New York: Peter Lang, 1992); Luther E. Smith Jr., *Howard Thurman: The Mystic as Prophet* (Richmond, IN: Friends United Press, 1991); Walter Earl Fluker and Catherine Tumber, eds., *A Strange Freedom: The Best of Howard Thurman on Religious Experience and Public Life* (Boston: Beacon Press, 1998). The University of South Carolina Press published the first two volumes of four of *The Papers of Howard Washington Thurman*, edited by Walter Fluker, in 2009 and 2012. See also Quinton Dixie and Peter Eisenstadt, *Visions of a Better World* (Boston: Beacon Press, 2011).

2. Howard Thurman, *With Head and Heart: The Autobiography of Howard Thurman* (New York: Harcourt Brace Jovanovich, 1979), 20–21.

3. Howard Thurman, ed., introduction to *A Track to the Water's Edge: The Olive Schreiner Reader*, by Olive Schreiner (New York: Harper and Row, 1973), xxvii–xxviii; Walter Fluker, ed., *The Papers of Howard Washington Thurman* (Columbia: University of South Carolina Press, 2009), 1:302–3.

4. Thurman, *With Head and Heart*, 73.

5. Ibid., 112–14.

6. Howard Thurman, *Why I Believe There Is a God: Sixteen Essays by Negro Clergymen with an Introduction by Howard Thurman* (Chicago: Johnson Publishing Company, 1965), xi.

7. Thurman, *With Head and Heart*, 134.

8. Fluker, *Papers of Howard Washington Thurman*, 1:302–3.

9. Howard Thurman, *Footprints of a Dream: The Story of the Church for the Fellowship of All Peoples* (New York: Harper and Brothers, 1959), 24.

10. Thurman, *With Head and Heart*, 129.

11. Thurman, *Footprints of a Dream*, 32.

12. For a detailed reconstruction of the visit to Gandhi, and writer and activist Mahadav Desai's account of the meeting, see Quinton Dixie and Peter Eisenstadt, *Visions of a Better World* (Boston: Beacon Press, 2011), reprinted in Fluker, *Papers of Howard Washington Thurman*, 1:332–39.

13. Lerone Bennett Jr., "Howard Thurman: 20th Century Holy Man," *Ebony* 33, no. 4 (February 1978): 76, 84.

14. Howard Thurman, *The Search for Common Ground* (New York: Harper and Row, 1973), 28.

15. Thurman, *Footprints of a Dream*, 24.

16. Ibid., 44.

17. Howard Thurman, *The Creative Encounter: An Interpretation of Religion and the Social Witness* (New York: Harper and Brothers, 1954), 20.

18. Howard Thurman, *Deep Is the Hunger: Meditations for Apostles of Sensitiveness* (New York: Harper and Brothers, 1951), 2.

19. Thurman, *Footprints of a Dream*, 76, 80.

20. Thurman, *Common Ground*, 76, 80.

21. Ibid., 82–83, 57–58.

22. Ibid., 67–68.

23. Ibid., 58.

24. Ibid., 67–68.

25. Ibid., 88.

26. Ibid., 92–93.

27. Ibid., 46–47.

28. Thurman, *With Head and Heart*, 245–47.

29. Ibid., 246–47.

30. Howard Thurman, *Meditations of the Heart* (Boston: Beacon Press, 1953), 211–12.

CHAPTER 5: THOMAS MERTON

1. Thomas Merton, *Seeds of Destruction* (New York: Farrar, Straus and Giroux, 1964), xiii.

2. Thomas Merton, *Passion for Peace: The Social Essays*, edited by William H. Shannon (New York: Crossroad, 1997), 2–3. The quotation is from Shannon's introduction. *Passion for Peace* includes the essays in "Part One: Black Revolution" in Merton, *Seeds of Destruction*, and several later essays by Merton on race.

3. Thomas Merton, *Conjectures of a Guilty Bystander* (Garden City, NY: Doubleday), 140–42.

4. Letter from Thomas Merton to Catherine de Hueck Doherty, December 6, 1941, in Thomas Merton, *The Hidden Ground of Love*, edited by William H. Shannon (New York: Farrar, Straus and Giroux, 1985), 10.

5. Paul Hanley Furfey, *Fire on the Earth* (New York: Macmillan, 1943), 51–52.

6. Merton, *Passion for Peace*, 163.

7. Thomas Merton journal entry, February 13, 1963, in Thomas Merton, *Turning toward the World: The Pivotal Years*, edited by Victor A. Kramer (New York: HarperCollins, 1996), 297.

8. Merton, *Seeds of Destruction*, 25.

9. Merton, *Passion for Peace*, 196.

10. Ibid., 289.

11. Thomas Merton, *The Courage for Truth: Letters to Writers* (New York: Farrar, Straus and Giroux, 1993), 244–45.

12. Thomas Merton, *Raids on the Unspeakable* (New York: New Directions, 1966), 15.

13. Ibid., 155.

14. Ibid., 169.

15. Ibid., 196.

16. Ibid., 191–92.

17. Ibid., 195.

18. Ibid., 174–75.

19. "Some Points from the Birmingham Nonviolence Movement," Abbey of Our Lady of Gethsemani, Trappist, Kentucky, June 10, 1964, in Davis W. Houck and David E. Dixon, eds., *Rhetoric, Religion, and the Civil Rights Movement, 1954–1965* (Waco, TX: Baylor University Press, 2006), 743–52.

20. Merton, *Passion for Peace*, 189–90.

21. Ibid., 187.

22. Merton, *Hidden Ground of Love*, 456–57.

23. Letter from Thomas Merton to W. H. Ferry, June 12, 1963, in ibid., 215.

24. Merton, *Passion for Peace*, 275.

25. Thomas Merton, *Ishi Means Man* (Greensboro, NC: Unicorn Press, 1976), 11.

26. Reprinted in Merton, *Passion for Peace*, 216.

27. Ibid., 183.

28. The entire letter was reprinted in Merton, *Passion For Peace*, 11–19. For quote, see ibid., 18–19.

CHAPTER 6: MARTIN LUTHER KING JR.

1. See Aldon D. Morris, *Origins of the Civil Rights Movement* (New York: Free Press, 1984).

2. A. J. Muste, "What the Bible Teaches about Freedom," in *The Essays of A. J. Muste*, ed. Nat Hentoff, 2nd ed. (New York: A. J. Muste Institute, 2001), 284.

3. Cited in Taylor Branch, *Parting the Waters: America in the King Years* (New York: Simon and Schuster, 1988), 889–92.

4. James M. Washington, ed., *A Testament of Hope: The Essential Writings and Speeches of Martin Luther King, Jr.* (San Francisco: Harper-Collins, 1991), 221–23.

5. Martin Luther King Jr., *Stride toward Freedom: The Montgomery Story* (New York: Harper and Row, 1958), 101–7.

6. The following account of the Selma campaign is drawn from Taylor Branch, *At Canaan's Edge: America in the King Years, 1965–68* (New York: Simon and Schuster, 2006); Charles E. Fager, *Selma 1965: The March That Changed the South* (Fayetteville, NC: Kimo Press, 2005); Sheyann Webb and Rachel West Nelson, *Selma, Lord, Selma: Childhood Memories*

of the Civil-Rights Days (Tuscaloosa: University of Alabama Press, 1980); Gustav Niebuhr, "Religion Journal; Remembering a Martyr in This Season of Hope," *New York Times*, April 8, 2000.

7. For quotes from Johnson's address to Congress on Selma, see Branch, *At Canaan's Edge*, 112–15.

8. For indispensable works on King's life, see David J. Garrow, *Bearing the Cross: Martin Luther King, Jr. and the Southern Christian Leadership Conference* (New York: William Morrow, 1986); Washington, *A Testament of Hope*; Branch, *Parting the Waters*. For Johnson's address to Congress on Selma, see Branch, *At Canaan's Edge*, 112–15.

9. Merton, *Seeds of Destruction*, xiii.

10. Cited in Garrow, *Bearing the Cross*, 58.

11. Thomas Merton, *Faith and Violence: Christian Teaching and Christian Practice* (Notre Dame, IN: University of Notre Dame Press, 1968), 130–31.

12. Cited in Washington, *Testimony of Hope*, 117.

13. Thomas Merton, *Seeds of Destruction* (New York: Farrar, Straus and Giroux, 1964), xiii.

14. Cited in Washington, *Testimony of Hope*, 240.

15. Thomas Merton, *Raids on the Unspeakable* (New York: New Directions, 1966), 15–16.

16. Cited in Washington *Testament of Hope*, 255.

17. Ibid., 119.

18. Ibid., 254.

19. Ibid.

20. William H. Shannon, ed., *The Hidden Ground of Love: The Letters of Thomas Merton on Religious Experience and Social Concerns* (New York: Farrar, Straus and Giroux, 1985), 451.

21. James Baldwin, *The Fire Next Time* (New York: Dial Press, 1963), 97.

CHAPTER 7: FANNIE LOU HAMER

1. Cited in Jerry DeMuth, "Tired of Being Sick and Tired," *Nation*, June 1, 1964, 549.

2. "Fannie Lou Hamer Speaks Out," *Essence*, October 1971, 53.

3. Ibid.

4. Cited in Meagan Parker Brooks, *A Voice That Could Stir an Army: Fanny Lou Hamer and the Rhetoric of the Black Freedom Movement* (Jackson: University Press of Mississippi, 2014), 17–18.

5. Cited in ibid., 54.

6. Cited in ibid., 53–54; DeMuth, "Tired of Being Sick and Tired," 549.

7. Fannie Lou Hamer, "Speech Delivered at Loop College, Chicago, Illinois, May 27, 1970," in *The Speeches of Fannie Lou Hamer: To Tell It Like It Is*, ed. Maegan Parker Brooks and Davis W. Houck (Jackson: University Press of Mississippi, 2011), 107. In an article she wrote in 1968, Hamer cited a parallel verse from Matthew 16:3 as the text for Bevel's sermon. Fannie Lou Hamer, "Sick and Tired of Being Sick and Tired," *Katallagete* 1, no. 8 (Fall 1968): 21.

8. "Fannie Lou Hamer, Interview," in John Egerton, *A Mind to Stay Here: Profiles from the South* (London: Macmillan, 1970), 97–98.

9. Brooks, *A Voice That Could Stir an Army*, 40.

10. Ibid.

11. Maegan Parker Brooks and Davis W. Houck, eds., *The Speeches of Fannie Lou Hamer: To Tell It Like It Is* (Jackson: University Press of Mississippi, 2011), 112–14.

12. Ibid., 4–6.

13. Fannie Lou Hamer, "Untitled Speech, Indianola, Mississippi, September 1964," in *Rhetoric, Religion, and the Civil Rights Movement, 1954–1965*, ed. Davis W. Houck and David E. Dixon (Waco, TX: Baylor University Press, 2006), 792. Extended quotation courtesy of Baylor University Press.

14. Fannie Lou Hamer, "To Praise Our Bridges," in *Mississippi Writers: Reflections of Childhood and Youth, Volume II: Nonfiction*, ed. Dorothy Abbott (Jackson: University Press of Mississippi, 1986), 326–27.

15. Cited in Kay Mills, *This Little Light of Mine: The Life of Fannie Lou Hamer* (New York: Dutton, 1993), 98.

16. Chana Kai Lee, *For Freedom's Sake: The Life of Fannie Lou Hamer* (Urbana: University of Illinois Press, 1999), 13; Mills, *This Little Light of Mine*, 98–99.

17. Fannie Lou Hamer, foreword to *Stranger at the Gates: A Summer in Mississippi*, by Tracy Sugarman (New York: Hill and Wang, 1966), vii–viii.

18. Brooks and Houck, *Speeches of Fannie Lou Hamer*, 44–45.

19. Ibid.

20. Lynne Olson, *Freedom's Daughters: The Unsung Heroines of the Civil Rights Movement from 1830 to 1970* (New York: Simon and Shuster, 2001), 320.

21. Harry Belafonte, with Michael Shnayerson, *My Song: A Memoir of Art, Race, and Defiance* (New York: Vintage, 2012), 293.

22. Cited in Mills, *This Little Light of Mine*, 171.

23. Lee, *For Freedom's Sake*, 147–49.

24. Brooks and Houck, *Speeches of Fannie Lou Hamer*, 118–20.

25. Ibid., 125.

26. Cited in Mills, *This Little Light of Mine*, 217; *Speeches of Fannie Lou Hamer*, 98–99; Lee, *For Freedom's Sake*, 166.

27. Hamer, "Sick and Tired of Being Sick and Tired," 19–26.

28. Howard Raines, *My Soul Is Rested* (New York: Penguin Books, 1983), 255.

29. Cited in Brooks, *A Voice That Could Stir an Army*, 251.

AFTERWORD

1. John W. O'Malley, *Four Cultures of the West* (Cambridge, MA: Harvard University Press, 2004), 74–75.

2. Sheyann Webb and Rachel West Nelson, *Selma, Lord, Selma: Childhood Memories of the Civil-Rights Days* (Tuscaloosa: University of Alabama Press, 1980), 117–18.

⌘ INDEX ⌘